MADRID/BARCELONA BY NIGHT

S I M O N & S C H U S T E R
A U S T R A L I A

FOR REVIEW

Publication/Embargo: _December_

Price: _$ 19.95_

For further information please contact:

GEORGINA CORNISH

Tel: 02-9415 9924

Please forward your review to:
Publicity Department
Simon & Schuster Australia
PO Box 507 East Roseville
NSW 2069

other cities in the **by Night** series

Frommer's

MADRID/BARCELONA
by Night

MADRID BY
JORDAN SIMON

BARCELONA BY
RICHARD SCHWEID
WITH CONTRIBUTIONS FROM
JORDAN SIMON

A BALLIETT & FITZGERALD BOOK
MACMILLAN • USA

a disclaimer

Prices fluctuate in the course of time, and travel information changes under the impact of the varied and volatile factors that influence the travel industry. Neither the author nor the publisher can be held responsible for the experiences of readers while traveling. Readers are invited to write to the publisher with ideas, comments, and suggestions for future editions.

about the authors

Jordan Simon has written several guidebooks, including *Irreverent Guide to the U.S. Virgin Islands* and the *Gousha/USA TODAY Ski Atlas*. He is also co-author of the *Celestial Seasonings Cookbook: Cooking With Tea*. Mr. Simon is a regular contributor to *Modern Bride*, *USAir Magazine*, *Caribbean Travel & Life*, *Atlanta Homes & Lifestyles*, and *Diversion* and has written on various topics for magazines including *Elle*, *Travel & Leisure*, *Town & Country*, *Los Angeles*, the *NY Times Syndicate*, and *Ski*.

Richard Schweid, a veteran journalist and the author of three books of creative nonfiction: *Hot Peppers*, *Catfish and the Delta*, and *Barcelona*. Presently a freelance journalist in Barcelona who writes regularly for the Associated Press, and a variety of publications. Also senior editor for the city's English-language monthly magazine, *Barcelona Metropolitan*.

Balliett & Fitzgerald, Inc.
Editorial director: Will Balliett
Executive editor: Tom Dyja
Production editor: Maria Fernandez
Associate editor: Sue Canavan
Editorial assistants: Rachel Florman, Margaret Hanscom, Aram Song, Ben Welch, and Paige Wilder

Macmillan Travel art director: Michele Laseau

MACMILLAN TRAVEL
A Simon & Schuster Macmillan Company
1633 Broadway
New York, NY 10019

ISBN 0-02-8618785
Library of Congress information available from Library of Congress.

special sales

Bulk purchases (10+ copies) of Frommer's and selected Macmillan travel guides are available to corporations, organizations, institutions, and charities at special discounts, and can be customized to suit individual needs. For more information write to Special Sales, Macmillan General Reference, 1633 Broadway, New York, NY 10019.

Manufactured in the United States of America

contents

MADRID BY NIGHT

what's
hot,
what's
not

Who but Ernest Hemingway would have written the perfect summation of Madrid nightlife? "To go to sleep at night in Madrid marks you as a little queer." After experiencing the non-stop "Irish wake" that is Madrid by night, you have to wonder if these people ever rest, let alone in peace. The national newspaper *El País* once reported that *madrileños* (the common Spanish term for residents of Madrid) actually require less sleep than other Spaniards (not to mention Europeans or Americans). Their data might be scientifically questionable, but it's empirically accurate. The locals call themselves *gatos* (cats) in ironic tribute to their nocturnal prowling, and their yowling (the decibel level in certain clubs has been verified as the world's loudest).

Just how obsessed are the madrileños with nightlife? When the right-wing Partido Popular (PP) assumed municipal power in the mid-eighties, it tried to crack down by closing bars at (for Madrid) the absurdly early time of 5am. Hard-core partyers devised a morbidly unique response to this "curfew": Hordes repaired to the funeral parlors and morgues surrounding the town hall—all of which are equipped with small bars to console mourners. After a hiatus, the PP again seized the reins of government in 1996. They've now adopted a more indirect, "conservative" approach, attempting to close the rowdier bars on trumped-up drug charges—or, more honestly, for unacceptable noise levels. After the earlier debacle, no one would dare pass a bill reforming the licensing and zoning laws. It's so easy to obtain a liquor permit in Madrid that the targeted clubs usually simply close for a week and reopen, if not in the same location, then elsewhere.

Madrileños have always loved to party. And after four decades of repression under Franco, there was an explosion on all levels, a creative and sociological ferment akin to that of the Beat fifties in Greenwich Village or of the Mod London sixties, each of which spawned its own style. To understand the unique style that emerged in Madrid in the eighties and the nineties you have to know something about "The Three Ms": *la movida, la madrugada,* and *la marcha.* Used to denote "movement" on many levels, *la movida* refers to the restlessness of the night crawlers, their craving for constant stimulation, drug-induced or otherwise. It's also the name of the artistic movement that lightened and brightened a drab, dreary city; one of la movida's leading representatives is internationally renowned filmmaker Pedro Almodóvar, who remains a fixture on the circuit. *La madrugada* means dawn, and most bars and clubs list their hours simply as "hasta la mad." Some like to point out that the "mad" scene that erupted after the long Franco night also indicated the dawn of a new era. Indeed. And while *la marcha* refers to the "march" of the night toward dawn, it's also used to express progress in other spheres—the economy, the arts, fashion, in short, the (over)hauling of an antiquated Spain in the last quarter of the 20th century.

The average Madrid nightspot hosts totally different crowds depending on the day and time. Still, certain bars and clubs do cater more to a particular type of clientele, and for that reason, there are three terms every visitor should know. There's the noun/adjective *pijo*, which translates as rich, snotty, snooty, haughty, hoity-toity, and as old as money gets in a formerly fascist nation. Then there's *la gente guapa*, which simply means beautiful people; here it's used less for the Concorde horde, though, than for the stand-and-pose model/celeb crowd. Finally, some places are thought of as *cutre*, which can be very roughly defined as "totally normal, dude." Mind you, in one of life's ironies, even the pijos have appropriated club style: the same dance mix, same street chic. Only the indefinable attitude—and the rigorous door policy—set their haunts apart. Otherwise, it seems perversely arbitrary: one bar is jammed at 1am, while its neighbor holds the ghostly hush of sudden evacuation. At 4am, the situation could be reversed. There's no rhyme or reason, as most bars and clubs seem virtually indistinguishable on the surface to the inexperienced observer. Decor favors black walls, pin lighting, and rock posters yellowed by years of cigarette smoke. The only apparent distinction is the music of choice; styles can range from ambient techno to acoustic guitar, from fifties rock and roll to reggae. And between the dim lighting, dense crowds, and even denser shroud of smoke (a combination of tobacco and hash), you can't see a thing anyway. (Asthmatics and/or claustrophobics, be warned!)

If you think you're being groped in a bar or club, take it neither as insult nor invitation. Actually, Spaniards, and madrileños in particular, are remarkably demonstrative. When it comes to PDAs (Public Demonstrations of Affection), Madrid blows Paris's rep as the "City of Love" right out of the Seine. Couples splay themselves across the hoods of cars, diddle in doorways, sit on one another's laps in the metro. Nearly every club has a section filled with high-backed couches for reclining (and very little declining). In gay bars, these rooms (usually outfitted with porn video screens) give way to a warren of back rooms where the action is decidedly less sedate. (As one bartender remarked, "You have to understand: Most of these men go home to their wives, mothers, or both—so where else can they go?")

The Madrid night crawl is a constantly evolving creature with a mind of its own. Although they remain staunchly loyal to their favorites, madrileños seem nonetheless unable to settle for a lengthy period in one place—a fear of commitment stemming from the fact that, *¿Quién sabe?*, the bar or club around the corner might be even more happening.

What's hot

Flamenco... For years madrileños shunned flamenco as an expression of the old-fashioned, backward Spain they sought to forget. There was also a racist component, as many trendoid *capitaleños* were ashamed of its Gypsy origins. Now that Spain has established a reputation as a "modern" country, flamenco is making a comeback, in part thanks to a new wave of musicians who have created a fusion of flamenco, jazz, reggae, blues, salsa, zouk, and pop called *nuevo flamenco*. Aficionados argue vehemently about whether this new amalgam represents a fresh reinterpretation or the subversion of an art form whose roots stretch back over 500 years; even today many traditionalists insist that *payos* (Gypsy slang for outsiders, even heathens) can never hope to understand its true, wild, maverick spirit. Even clubs specializing in *flamenco puro* have also zoomed in popularity. Forget the clichéd image of clicking castanets, stomping heels, roses in teeth, tambourines, and black lace mantillas. Flamenco refers not only to the dance, but also to the music itself. The songs, called *cante jondo*, spiral from joyous, defiant declarations of love to wailing laments for its loss. The musical styles include familiar names like tango, fandango, and malagueñas, as well as *tarantos, tientos, alegrías, seguidillas, soleares,* and *bulerías,* each of which has its own unique rhythm, regional origin, and lyrical substance. As with listening to anything in an unfamiliar tongue, the songs can sometimes seem grating, resembling the sharp sounds of a restless half-sleep, like yowling toms. Yet there's something thrillingly dramatic, even undeniably hypnotic about the experience; a great singer, with only his or her acoustic guitar for accompaniment, can place an audience in a trance. As a matter of fact, this magical spell, called *duende*, is the ultimate aim, uniting artist and audience. In its purest expression, flamenco is every bit as primal, even cathartic, as that other classic Andalusian tradition, bullfighting, and it requires just as much showmanship and dexterity. There are two types of flamenco club: the *tablao flamenco* and the *sala rociera* (for recommendations, see The Club Scene). The former stages shows, often with leading artists, that are usually rather spectacular in scale. The latter are generally smaller venues that might present live acts, but also allow audience participation—the flamenco version of karaoke—with sometimes hilarious results.

Lavapiés and La Latina... These two solidly working class neighborhoods have become home to some of Madrid's trendier bars, clubs, and restaurants, a perfect example of the inverse snobbism that has infected the city. Just as in Manhattan, more than half the locals originally came from somewhere else. These gentrified nabes have traditionally been the bastions of the *castizos,* the Madrid equivalent of cockneys, right down to their penchant for rhyming slang and endearing arrogance.

Almodóvar colors... While Madrid practically takes filmmaker Pedro Almodóvar for granted (after all, they've enjoyed his sexy film comedies for over a decade now), his bold Dayglo colors remain all the rage in clubs. Lavender and orange are fashion Do's, whether on your hair or your vinyl panties. And when the clubs themselves aren't black or beige, they're splashed in lipstick and nail polish hues like cherry red and tangerine.

Gay chic... Madrileños are remarkably sensitive to their image throughout the world. They desperately want to be perceived as chic, fashionable, au courant, PC. That's why Almodóvar is worshipped as a hero; he almost singlehandedly popularized Madrid as the hip, hopping, happening place to be. It's also why gays and lesbians—and their almost stereotypical sense of style in clothes and dance music—have achieved unprecedented acceptance. That's not to say that Catholic—not catholic—Spain thoroughly welcomes the idea of homosexuality. This remains a country where the phrase "God knows" is still de-blasphemed to read *"¿Quién sabe?"* (*who* knows?) in movie subtitles. But many gay and lesbian nightspots have become known as stylish hangouts for the straight and terminally cool, and in the predominantly gay Chueca district no one bats an eyelash, overly mascara-ed or not, when men kiss openly in the streets.

Anything American... What Jack Lang, then French Minister of Culture, decried back in the seventies as "coca-colonization," has inundated Madrid in a tidal wave of American consumerism (and consumer goods). Just as cultural protectionism has become outré among Parisians, madrileños have devoured anything and everything American. It starts with the merchandising: they've caught Nike fever and sport baseball caps (worn backwards, of course). And the number of McDonald's, Burger Kings, and similar franchises has nearly doubled in the nineties—not counting the Mexican *taquerías* and Madrid's own *bocadillerías* (the Spanish equivalent of Subways), some of which remain open late for a quick fix between clubs. The Hard Rock Cafe is just as jammed as its counterparts around the globe, and Planet Hollywood will probably zoom into orbit when it opens in 1998. Worst of all is the explosion of faux-Western "saloons," rib joints, and fifties kitsch diners. What's next? Elvis sightings?

What's not

Machismo... As part of Spain's generalized modernization movement, overt machismo—that swaggering Latino display of testosterone—is now considered in poor taste. Most madrileños wouldn't dream of harassing a single woman. Mind you, the men are still a tad possessive, placing a "hands off" palm on their girlfriends' butts, or parading them about like runway models. But if they haven't yet exactly embraced the concept of the "sensitive" man, they've certainly gone a long way toward accepting women as their equals in the workplace. Perhaps the most despised symbol of the "old" ways are the *tunas,* folkloric bands of troubadours that ostentatiously trace their origins to the 12th century. They strut about in traditional torero-style period costume, replete with puffed sleeves, serenading foreign señoritas (whether they like it or not). The *tunos* (individual singers) have entree to most of the touristy establishments around the Plaza Mayor and Plaza Santa Ana, where they strum their guitars, sing off-key, and get plastered. The scariest thing is that these guys actually think they're hot stuff. So, should a fellow in crimson sashes sashay up to you, remember this: they're not poor little lambs, just wolves in cheap clothing.

Plaza Mayor... As if "traditions" like the tunas and inflated prices weren't enough to drive you away, you'll also have to cope with the hordes of tourists clucking and clicking away (your average cheesy tuno will say "Cheese!" in a Kodak moment). By all means, visit the Plaza Mayor, which remains one of Europe's most ravishing squares (despite the bizarrely hallucinogenic murals the government commissioned to 'decorate' it). And take a peek at the surrounding maze of picturesque side streets. You could even indulge in a drink, watching the living theater (at times of the absurd) parade by. But don't make it the hub of your stay, not if you want to encounter the real Madrid.

Pick-up scenes... Just like machismo itself, the blatant pass is passé in Madrid. Part of what's behind this is the reaction against traditional macho attitudes. Another part is that Catholic upbringing. And in truth, madrileños are ultimate romantics who believe in courtship, even if it's only by the hour. If you watch carefully, you'll realize that most people in the bars are coupled. Of course, cruising does go on, especially in gay clubs—boys will be boys and girls girls. But in general, if you want to pick someone up, at least indulge in some light flirtation first–and consider offering dinner. One exception is bars that cater to *guiris* (local argot for "hick tourists," but meant affectionately), many of them located in the vicinity of Plaza Santa Ana and Calle Huertas. You just know you'll find some dishy/hunky local looking to seduce the willing with his or her sexy accent. Should you find yourself entertaining back in your hotel room, remember it's surprisingly difficult to find condoms late at night; if you're not prepared, better make sure your partner is. As one of the brasher local sayings goes, *"No digas que no a la una, a lo que digas que sí a las tres, y por lo que serías capaz de pagar a las cinco."* Translation: "Don't say no at 1am to something you'd say yes to at 3 and pay for at 5."

the club scene

Disco bowling…aquatic aerobics…the latest dance mix…the madrileños are on a never-ending quest for the vampire's Holy Grail: something new and different to sink their teeth into. Decadence, even depravity, are often par for the course. And while the repressive pall of Franco's regime might have passed 20 years ago, the restless Gypsy spirit of la movida (see What's Hot, What's Not) that burst forth at that time with orgasmic intensity still informs the frenzied, frenetic pace of the city's nightlife.

Clubs hip-hop in and out of vogue in Madrid, yet every local seems to have uncanny radar for the spot of the moment. This helps explain the wildly diverse crowds at many venues (some of which are no larger than a studio apartment in Manhattan). And the clubs themselves are as varied as the club crowds: While many of the old-fashioned dance halls—where the tango, foxtrot, and waltz are executed with élan by the silver-haired set—are still holding out, if you want discos with attitude, you've also come to the right place. Some of the clubs today are clearly shrines to the latest waves of 'indie' music. Some specialize in traditional forms like jazz and flamenco. Others, however, change their name and identity nightly: Tonight at 3am it's the grunge/safety-pin crowd, but tomorrow at 6am it's techno/slumming yuppie time! (And as long as we're discussing variety, be sure to scan The Bar Scene chapter for venues that have live music, and, unlike the places in this chapter, charge no cover.)

Madrid *is* vampire Valhalla. To begin with, the admission prices are hardly steep—usually 600 to 1,500 ptas., or $5–$12. (The exceptions are the joints with the big-name performers and the flamenco clubs, some of which include dinner in the price.) But that entry fee also buys you a free drink, your choice of anything from a plain old *cerveza* to a healthy shot of vodka, depending on how schnockered you want to get. Another nice thing about Madrid's clubs is that, aside from being able to tango or pasodoble up a storm, madrileños are not known for their sense of rhythm, even if they *are* beautiful. Any computer geek can look like Travolta on a Madrid dancefloor.

Getting Past the Velvet Rope

First things first: remember it just *won't* do to show up too early—madrileños may have invented the term fashionably late (though they're unfailingly punctual for personal appointments). But even if you do insist on arriving before the crowds converge, you still might not get in if you don't have the right look. And at many clubs, you might actually have to run the gauntlet twice—first past the bouncers, then by the cashiers, who look even more eager to cashier you. They have the final word and can show you the door even if the doormen didn't slam it in your face.

So what is the right dress code? Well, ever since the days of Franco, madrileños have tried to cultivate a sophisticated image. At the same time, no one wants to be perceived as pijo (slang for rich, haughty, snotty)—except of course the pijos themselves. Although Madrid has its share of fashion fascists, even the piss-elegant places no longer have a specific dress code. That being said, however, style is essential—that had better be a designer black leather jacket and those boots had better be Ferragamos! Only in the handful of more old-fashioned dance halls and discos are jacket and evening dress still expected (see Lowdown below).

The rest of the nightcrawlers sport a standard uniform. Second-hand, ill-fitting clothes are the norm, though many men and women still choose to display their wares (usually with good reason). So break out those checked Buddy Holly-ish or scarlet leather capri pants, or at least wrap a sweatshirt around your jeans like a skirt. Wear unflattering colors like dung, or, at the opposite end of the spectrum, go psychedelic. Gals, torn fishnet stockings work. Guys, studded leather jackets are great, and if you can wear your hair long without resembling a youthful Tiny Tim (most madrileños can't), you're there.

And remember, madrileños *love* accessories. Safety pins in denim jackets are good, even better in parts of your anatomy. Biker accoutrements—a discreetly placed chain or two—are way cool. Don't neglect the footwear: combat boots, hiking shoes, Reeboks, and Nikes, preferably scuffed. Hair? Spikes and mohawks are out. That clean-cut, retro fifties look now prevails for guys (you know, 90210 side-burns); military buzz cuts also command attention, for both sexes. Ladies, whatever you do, just don't seem too 'coiffed,' even if it does cost you a hundred bucks at the salon to perfect that unstyled, just-out-of-bed look. Unless, of course, you're at that age when diamonds don't look preten-tious; the lacquered look never went out of style for those over 45 in Madrid.

Oh, one last thing, especially if you don't speak Spanish: Latch and leech onto a local if you can. Madrileños pride themselves on knowing everyone on their "rounds" or at least fast-talking their way in (without resorting to name-dropping). Veterans of the night always manage to look and sound as if they belong. If you can't adopt a personal guide but you *habla* even semi-fluently, it never hurts to assume an assured yet not truculent "Yeah? Doesn't matter who I am: Just who the hell do you think *you* are?" attitude with the intimidators. That's "*¿Sí? No importa quien soy yo, pero ¿quién carajo te crees que eres tú?*"

Timing

Unless otherwise noted, dance and music clubs are generally open from about 10pm until dawn on weekends and until at least 4am weeknights. Exceptions are the Latin, classical, and jazz clubs and the tablaos flamencos, which close by 3 or 4am every night. The dance halls are usually open by 8 or 9pm and close around 2am weeknights, 5am weekends. Some discos and dance halls also have early-evening sessions on weekends. After-hours joints don't open their doors before 5am. Most shows don't begin until 11:30, and sets can start as late as 2, even 3am. Check the indispensable weekly entertainment guide *Guía del Ocio* for complete listings as well as cover charges.

Despite Madrid's anything-goes spirit, the nightly version of la marcha is actually quite a regimented ritual in its way. The after-work drink is usually sipped at a neighborhood-style bar. This segues into tapas time at a café (or *mesón* or *taberna* or *tasca* or *cervecería* or *sidrería*...), roughly between 8 and 10:30pm, when it's time for dinner. Next the typical Madrileño ventures either to a sleek, chic boîte (occasionally called a cocktail bar or *cocktelería*), or to hear live music in a disco-bar (it's not what we would call a disco, though it might have a postage-stamp–sized dance floor, people gyrating atop the bar itself, and gorillas at the door with 'tude to spare'). Barring that, they might take in a flamenco performance, a cabaret act in the larger, old-fashioned dance halls, or a spectacular revue at a *sala de fiesta*. Nobody, but nobody, enters a *discoteca* (the kind replete with flashing lights, crystal balls, and even cage dancers) before 3am.

Around daybreak they emerge like the walking dead and enter a *chocolatería* or *churrería* (which sells *churros*, fried dough rings similar to beignet spirals). It's time for a pick-me-up coffee, usually with a hefty splash of anisette or cognac (known as a *carajillo*). If you're not in need of an intravenous dose of caffeine by this point, order a *sol y sombra*—brandy and anisette minus the coffee; the Spaniards refer to this as *matar el gusanillo* (killing the worm). Then, at 6 or 7am, it could be pick-up time, especially on weekends, and especially at the untamed after-hours clubs.

Clubs in Central Madrid

Al Andalus **5**
Al Lab 'Oratorio **10**
Amadís **4**
Angels of Xenon **37**
Aqualung Madrid **31**
Bali Hai **19**
Bocaccio **8**
But **12**
Café Central **35**
Café de Chinitas **20**
Café del Foro **1**
Café del Mercado **32**
Canciller **6**
Casa Patas **36**
Chaquetón **33**
Clamores **2**
Cleofás **7**
Corral de la Morería **29**
Down **15**
Empire **9**
Goa **45**
Golden Gran Vía **28**
Heaven **22**
Honky Tonk **3**
Joy Eslava **26**
Kabul **21**
Kathmandu **27**
Maravillas **14**
Midnight **17**
Morocco **18**
Nature **17**
Pachá **11**
Palace **24**
Palacio de Gaviria **25**
Pasapoga **44**
Populart **39**
El Refugio **34**
La Rosa **42**
Shangay Tea Dance **45**
Siroco **16**
El Sol **43**
La Soléa **30**
Stella **41**
Strong Center **23**
Suristán **40**
Swing **13**
Teatro Kapital **38**

Church †
Information ⓘ
Metro Ⓜ
Post Office ✉

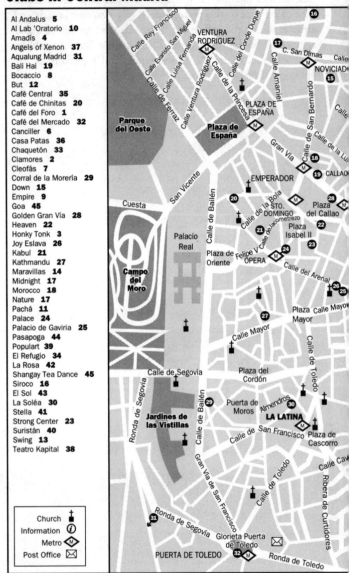

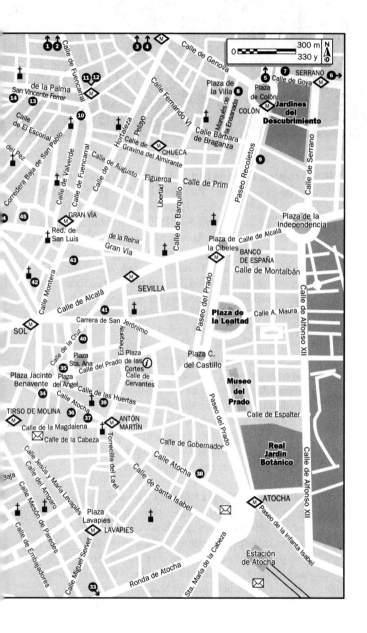

Hip-hopping happening... Resembling a garage sale from a long-closed Trader Vic's, **Bali Hai** bills itself as a "boîte tropical," which conveys its laughably un-PC personality: paper Chinese lanterns, fake Polynesian thatching, Easter Island–style carvings, flaming torches, even a Chinese lion guarding the entrance (along with a couple of mean-looking bouncers, studiedly surly in leather and chains). The carpets may be soiled and the seats torn, but go figure: This is the steamiest spot in town for hip-hop, trip-hop, and jolting jungle sounds. The crowd leans toward slumming yuppies and college kids entirely in black. An eclectic set comes to **Morocco** for the hipper-than-thou ambience and pulsing percussive mix of hard-core industrial, techno, and metal, though Thursday nights' House of Devotions remains devoted to house and hip-hop. Expect to see tattooed ladies in torn lace stockings, club kids in shorts (even in the dead of winter), computer nerds in baggy checked pants, retro punks with scarlet and indigo mohawks, even the occasional suit. Flashing red lights and faux leopard-skin seats complete the Almodóvar ambience.

Not as cool as they claim... Okay, with its cushy sofas (great for necking), smoked glass mirrors, chandeliers, and red velvet curtains, **Joy Eslava** is gorgeous. And the DJs do know how to put the right spin on the evening, so that you're almost willing to overlook all the roving eyes (and hands) and the fact that there as many English speakers as Spanish speakers here. But for all its renovated 19th-century pomp and pretension, this is still a 'Hey, baby, what's your sign?' kinda place. With its snob appeal, mannequin-like pijos, yet undistinguished music and decor, **Empire** defines overrated. The space itself is hardly remarkable: a crowded dance floor and a balcony to survey the scene. Attractive curvy hand-carved maroon columns provide the only notable design flourish. For all its flash and glitz (the usual brass and glass), the old-fashioned dance hall **Amadís** is frozen in the era of the beehive and bouffant, which could almost apply to the men, who are so vain they seem to think those rugs are Persian. They'd do better with their companions' fake furs. The doormen are downright rude to anyone under 40 who doesn't fit the profile.

Casting your net for castanets... Café de Chinitas appears to provide the Disneyesque version of flamenco, right down to the haute bordello decor (red velour, brass, faux gas lamps, marble halls, bull sculpture, decorously draped mantillas, even busts of famous flamenco artists), but the house troupe is well regarded. Join the mature *turista* crowd for the drinks and show—dinner offers only a simple menu (grilled prawns, roast chicken, veal scalloppine) that manages to be overcooked as well as overpriced. The space is so lush, even the windows have ornate wrought-iron guards (perhaps to prevent unsuspecting tourists from escaping once they get their stratospheric bill). Chinita's main competitor for glitz and comfort, **Corral de la Morería**, puts on a "rilly big shoe," as Ed Sullivan used to say. Everything feels authentic, from the wood beams and columns to the hand-painted chairs to the crisply starched, stuffed-shirt waiters. **Al Andalus** draws a discriminating older crowd, many of whom hail from Andalucia, as does the decor, with its Mudejar arches, flowerpots, stucco walls, Sevilla china plates, and tile floors). The intimate setting immediately establishes an affinity between *cantaores* (balladeers) and audience, creating a highly charged atmosphere in which hand-clapping and olé-ing mount to a fever pitch. Ask most madrileños and they'll tell you **Casa Patas** is the most authentic tablao flamenco in town (Brits have been heard to comment rather dubiously, "It's so real you can smell it," though that's probably a reference to the glorious garlic aroma of the marvelous food.) The look is perfect: intricate tile floors, red-and-white checked tablecloths, high-back wood chairs that encourage ramrod posture, pictures of flamenco artists, and graceful wrought-iron colonnades. While emphasizing tradition, Casa Patas also books top nuevo flamenco artists; you could spend several nights here familiarizing yourself with the rituals—and first families—of flamenco. Friday nights are SRO at **Chaquetón**, the city's most popular *peña* (a tiny, not-for-profit clubs dedicated to preserving the traditions of *flamenco puro*). This place attracts the top artists—and most fervent aficionados of all ages. As the performance progresses, the entire audience begins to clap and stomp in unison, and the ancient building shakes like L.A. during a quake. Be forewarned, however: the ventilation is dreadful, the smoke has nowhere to go, there are no eats or seats, and in summer it gets hotter than the music itself. The patrons wouldn't have it any other way. **La Soléa** is a smallish room with classic Sevilla tile work and black-and-white photos of agonized-looking flamenco artists. Come around 2am when the place is packed and everyone's plastered and the habitués are wrestling for the open mike; the wailing and caterwauling must be heard to be believed. But just when you're about to put your fingers in your ears, there's that inevitable magic moment when someone delivers a *cante jondo* of such ferocious feeling that the entire rowdy room becomes as still as a church.

For techno or metal... The clientele at the trippy-looking, Oriental-inspired **Kathmandu** runs the gamut: shaved heads to pony tails, rugby Ts to leather vests, black vinyl dresses and magenta granny glasses to flesh-colored body suits ripped to expose tattoos of intricate Bosch-like scenes. Androgyny qualifies as a major lifestyle here. The bar on the top floor features Tibetan textiles draped from the ceiling like a sultan's tent; downstairs, odd metal sculptures entangled in nets and Nepalese art provide a vivid contrast to the cantaloupe walls and multi-arched ceiling. The throbbing mix is techno, acid jazz, and industrial with just a wee bit of grunge, and dancers jerk about on the impossibly crowded floor like the first generation of robots. At **Maravillas** the DJs rock in their booth as if on speed, and the barely legal crowd favors multiple piercings, including the latest bones in vogue. The bands here are as wild and uninhibited as the audience. Strobe lighting, Star Wars videos on a loop, and the scent of... something special in the air make it the nineties version of an acid trip. Whatever you do, keep dancing to the scrupulously up-to-the-minute techno/house/ambient/industrial/gothic beat at **Midnight** (aka

Nature on Thursdays). The decor is totally *nada* (concrete slabs, chipped paint everywhere, and slightly raised platforms surrounding the dance floor), the seat cushions are dirty, even sticky, and much of the hygienically-challenged crowd lends a new definition to the term airing your dirty laundry. **Canciller** is the place for metal so heavy it isn't on the periodic table. Everything is black here: the walls, the clothes, even the lights. And it's a little creepy, since everyone—from the burly bikers to the skinny skinheads—looks either angry or doped out. It's also unbelievably loud and, natch, smoky.

All that jazz... **Clamores** means noises in Spanish, but only the silkiest of syncopations prevail at this sizable venue where you can also hear ethnic sounds from around the world. Wallowers in luxe will also appreciate one of Madrid's widest selections of *cava* (sparkling wine) and the stylish surroundings: ochre walls painted with musical notes, mirrored columns, and marble tables. The fare at **Café Central** tends to be more traditionalist, in keeping with its faded fin-de-siècle decor and ambience (oak wainscoting, brass, mirrors, etched and stained glass, marble tables). Such notables as Don Pullen, Jean-Pierre Rampal, Wynton Marsalis, and George Adams do gigs here for a demanding, musically erudite audience. The club is perennially rated by the jazz rags as one of Europe's best. Despite the name, **Populart** has a certain purist rigor about its acts and atmosphere. In many ways, it almost feels like a Greenwich Village club circa 1959: the decor is mostly severe black and white, and you half expect a bunch of beatniks to break out in an Apache dance. Jazz acts here tend to be local.

Toughest doors to crack... For all you know, the dressy gorillas at **Empire** might be packing heat, as this is a favored spot for the royal family and its eye-catching retinue. Given the club's tony address, it's no surprise that this otherwise nondescript space also hosts special events like fashion shows and music-industry functions. The techno temple **Nature** is the definition of inverse snobbism: The more indigent and menacing you look (shaved heads, piercings, and tattoos are practically de rigueur for both sexes), the better your chances of getting past the truly scuzzy doormen. Steel hand on velvet rope aptly describes

THE CLUB SCENE ⟨ THE LOWDOWN

the door policy at **Pachá**, a playpen for *la gente guapa*, the violently beautiful and merely wealthy. The nearly as well-bred doormen stand like sentinels, and there are more private rooms here than Studio 54 had in its heyday. Everything, from the decor to the clientele, is class (as in "ruling") all the way. Even the entrance areas are chic, with their aqua sofas, gilt mirrors, huge potted plants, silver art deco doors with leather padding, and tasteful paintings; a stunning domed ceiling over the main dance floor completes the picture. **Amadís** is easily the snobbiest of the dance halls (the doormen inspect your shoes with the avidity of foot fetishists, lest your boots scuff their precious floors). It may be 7am but your eyes should remain as white as your teeth if you want to experience seductive **Bocaccio**. The doormen are selective but the customers are even choosier; even when they're dancing wildly at 6am to a pulsating gothic/industrial mix, they never seem to work up a sweat.

Where the girls are... Don't be fooled by the curvy, frilly elegance at the intimate **La Rosa**. The action can get wild as the ladies let their hair (or what there is of it) down. A perfect example: one woman, her butch-styled do dyed blacker-than-black, eyes kohled until they resemble deep bruises, Dietrich-like legs sheathed in black silk stockings that stop just short of her pelvis, distractedly fans her crotch as she surveys the action. There are plenty of nooks and crannies for romantic petting, and most of the women are happily coupled on the dance floor. **Angels of Xenon** is so anything-goes that it's the only "gay" disco where women, lesbian or straight, are not merely welcome but an indispensable part of the fun.

Where the boys are... To call **Angels of Xenon** a gay disco (it's virtually straight before 2am) would be missing the point; it's simply a must stop on the Grand Tour of Madrid Nightlife. The drag shows are, to pun on the French, *comme il faux*. The queens here are poured into spandex dresses or robotic costumes that look extremely uncomfortable (and they must be sweltering under those moving laser track lights), but these 'girls' are pros, baby, as are the edible go-go boys who cater to their every whim. Sunday's **Shangay Tea Dance** at **Goa** is one helluva good time, whatever your sexual orientation. Women are welcome—and not all of them are lesbians. The rather gothic decor—orange walls with vermilion accents, purple lights draped in netting, and gold-topped black and hand-painted columns embedded in the walls—is the perfect backdrop to Madrid's most outrageous drag shows. Why is the dance floor always deserted at **Strong Center**? As one bartender jokes, it's because "the back-room area is larger than Santiago Bernabeu Stadium." The first of these rooms is lined with toilet stalls. Prospectors prowl the perimeter, persistently trying to make meaningful eye contact, even though it's so dark that only the occasional flare of a cigarette illuminates the men nonchalantly leaning against the stalls. Venture farther back and you find a porn video salon with the requisite high-back sofas. Then comes the pièce de resistance—the grope room, where guys flick their lighters to check out the action. **Kabul** is the choice of the harder-core leather crowd; a strict dress code is enforced for 'Cock Ring Night' on Thursdays. Slave masks, studded dog collars, and mesh panties also go over well here. The top floor is pool tables, stripper posters, and Tom of Finland–style murals of bulging, uniformed men; there's even a motorcycle in case you didn't get the point. Oddly enough there are comfy if ratty sofas for chatting (or making out passionately). The deliriously over-the-top **El Refugio** looks like the kind of place where Caligula might have enjoyed tossing about in his salad days. The interior is designed to resemble a grotto, with sensuous, sinuous Gaudíesque curves galore and nude gladiator statues. Glazed go-go boys dance dispassionately in cages while the sweaty crowd refuses to shed its leather no matter what.

Where to hear local bands... Few clubs anywhere exert as much influence on the local music scene as **Siroco**, which even has its own record label and newsletter. It showcases Spain's top indie performers, many of them heavily influenced by UK alternative rock, powerfully raw and so cutting-edge they practically draw blood. The bands' names alone are entertaining: Petersellers, Agua de Iguana + Joker, Hot Milk, Dibi Dibok. Its two rooms sport psychedelic colors: one hot pink and jade, the other orange and black, with everyone bathed in savagely red lighting. **Maravillas** is one of the trendier indie hangouts in the Malasaña neighborhood, booking mostly ambient, techno, and trance bands. The decor is suitably hallucinogenic, with bongo drums and Guatemalan-style murals, as well as a very disturbing painting of four guys in sunglasses diddling with their instruments (sounds innocent but see it for yourself). Probably Madrid's finest venue for ethnic sounds, **Suristán** books exciting young acts in rock, acid jazz, reggae, Brazilian, flamenco, funk, African fusion, and more. Exposed brick, gray or black marble tables, creamsicle walls, conical metal lamps, candelabras, and African masks give it a classier ambience than most venues. One big perk is the CDs and tapes sold in the front room, usually for that night's artist, but also for related acts. At **Al Lab'Oratorio**, the owners take pride in introducing fresh talent, often via advertised "War-of-the-Bands" nights. It's shockingly comfy, even smart (comparatively speaking): cool painted tables and a gorgeous carved wood bar in front, abstract pastels and frescoes of guitars and musical scales in the back, and Carnival costumes and African masks in odd corners of the downstairs performance space. The magnificent acoustics and up-and-coming Spanish bands like Dr. Explosion and Maralians attract a knowledgeable, fun, youthful bunch to the dilapidated but beloved **El Sol**. It's somewhat seedy, with tattered yellow and pink curtains everywhere and a spiral staircase rimmed with elephantine bare white bulbs. Strangely, most of the waiters are old enough to be the patrons' parents: they even wear classically cut burgundy jackets and lace shirts, which adds an almost surreal touch.

Latino, Castilian-style... Part of a disastrous attempt to convert a fish market into a swanky shopping center at the edge of town (the faux oak paneling clashes drastically with the iron bars lined with mirrors and crystal blue bottles), **Café del Mercado** has managed to stay open thanks to its uniformly excellent line-up of Latino artists. The cathedral ceiling guarantees fine acoustics and the sight lines are first-rate. **Café del Foro** overdoes the amour ambience, with slightly prissy decor including Roman colonnades (hence the name) and a starry sky painted above the stage. But the acts are serious indeed, with superior bolero, salsa, and merengue.

After hours... Opulent **Bocaccio** is the ultimate in afterhours decadence, with Madrid's sexiest crowd (and don't they know it). The downstairs area is nicknamed *Infierno* (Hell) for its intense scarlet decor and steamy make-out sessions on plush red velour Victorian sofas. The upstairs is only slightly less extravagant, with tapestries, soft green silk-and-metal lamps, and antique love seats. The music, when it's not techno/industrial, ranges from Depeche Mode to Pet Shop Boys on a loop (Britpop is très chic in Madrid). On weekends, **Down** is anything but. Large as it is, it's still always cheek-by-jowl (or cheek-by-cheek) with trance dancers shaking (in some cases, getting the shakes) to a phenomenal funk and soul mix. At dank but gaudy **Goa**, all the boys are as gaunt, pale, and emaciated as El Greco saints (albeit clad in Metallica T-shirts), while two of their girlfriends would fit into one zaftig Goya *Naked Maja*. Techno, gothic, ambient, and house rule, though there are also extended, surreal riffs into eighties Britpop and seventies metal. Attention-deficit disorderlies, butt-master babes, and club kids in khaki camouflage flock to **Heaven**. There are several levels, dramatically different from each other. One area has a long, sleek gray marble bar, blue neon, mirrored tables, masks, mesh-and-metal furnishings, and angels. Another more intimate bar has exquisite wainscoting and a Toulouse Lautrec–like painted ceiling. Still another resembles a gentleman's library, with old wood plank floors, faded velour sofas, and hunting prints.

Strictly ballroom... But (that's its name) is where the not-quite-beautiful-enough crowd goes when they can't get into the wildly popular **Pachá** down the block. Though Top 40 is occasionally spun, But is perhaps the most chic ballroom dance hall in Madrid, playing everything from Latin to big band. The crowd—mostly professional types in their 30s and 40s—can take free lessons earlier in the evenings in virtually every kind of touch dance, including tango, pasodoble, rumba, samba, chachacha, swing, and salsa. What sets the vaguely deco **Palace** apart is a gimmick straight from the 1930s Kit Kat Club in *Cabaret:* period-style telephones at 36 of the 125 tables. See someone you like but fear rejection face-to-face? Ring table 15 and say, "Hi, I'm (fill in name), wanna dance?" This sweet, old-fashioned touch usually guarantees results. On the fabulous mirrored stage, slinky women clad in clingy black dresses or form-fitting gold lamé hot pants and lace tank tops belt and bop about to live Spanish pop from the excellent orchestra. 50-somethings virtually tango down the lighted staircase at **Pasapoga** into an old-fashioned flashy, splashy space with marble floors, elephantine crystal chandeliers, brass fixtures, red velour sofas, gold lamé curtains, and mirrors—kind of a sixties take on a turn-of-the-century cat house. Fancy attire (suit and tie and long dresses) is a must; even the staff is tuxedoed. A different revue is mounted every night; most—gasp!—even show a little skin, some of it male.

Blues in the night... As the name suggests, **Honky Tonk** specializes in blues, rockabilly, fifties rock, R&B, and country-and-western. Despite the name, it's not a good idea to show up in your scuffed cowboy boots and a ten-gallon hat. This is a high-tech, fairly tony club that caters to your basic upscale down-home clientele. It's very touristy, very yuppie, and very popular. On weekends, an enthusiastic crowd packs **Siroco** to groove to nostalgic tracks from the sixties ('Retha, Ike & Tina, Marvin Gaye, and Earth, Wind & Fire) and seventies (disco divas Gloria Gaynor and Donna Summer). Dig the cool digs: the Blues Brothers stenciled on the door and a mural of Euro-African men and women in bellbottoms and platform heels, toting revolvers—sort of like stills from a blaxploitation flick.

And now for something completely different... The entrance of **Aqualung Madrid**—all crimson and gilt—is deceptively smart, until you reach the painfully well-lit pizza and burger stands straight from Coney Island. The interior, complete with swimming pools and 'canals,' resembles a YMCA health club crossbred with a tacky small-town disco. The stench of chlorine (plus that inimitably musty locker room aroma) pervades the entire multilevel complex. If you strike out trying to pick someone up at the otherwise tired disco **Stella**, you can always pick up a strike or a spare: The dance areas occupy balconies surrounding four bowling lanes. All the rage in the early nineties, this one-joke club has enjoyed its 15 minutes of fame—unless, of course, you really do favor the musical menu, which leans toward sixties mod London sounds like the Stones and the Kinks. **Teatro Kapital**, more amusement park than disco, is a world unto itself: It includes a movie room, snack bar, karaoke bar, an iguana house, pool tables, even candy machines and an automatic teller. Each of its seven floors sports unique decor from *Bladerunner* futuristic to Gaudíesque.

For 30-somethings who don't want to be... The ornate **Palacio de Gaviria** set in an actual 19th-century palace, is so swooningly exquisite and kindly lit that chivalry no longer seems dead and age seems to vanish from everyone's happy face. It's probably the most romantic disco in the world—you could probably pop the question here. With truly hip DJs, stunning decor, and just enough attitude at the door, **Joy Eslava** fulfills the need for those out of their clubbing diapers to feel fashionable and wanted. Back in the eighties, **Swing** was one of the citadels of la movida. Now it caters mostly to folks in their 30s and 40s who didn't live la movida and want desperately to catch up. It's also known as a weekend pick-up joint. The club affects a half-hearted art deco look, with leaded glass and brass mirrors that contrast with floors that don't seem to have been swept, let alone scrubbed, in a decade. Nonetheless, it remains a fine venue for traditional Spanish pop, including *cantaores,* and cabaret. Depending on the night, the taped music runs the gamut from ballroom to bebop, salsa to swing.

For 40- and 50-somethings... Despite the hard-edged glitz of its decor—strobe lights, a ceiling layered with ball-bearings, chandeliers dripping with crystal daggers—**Cleofás** is the kind of place where women travel in packs and pout at the men they fancy. Gentlemen of a certain age and carriage approach a table of three señoritas (probably divorced, and of a certain age and bearing) with, *"Oye! Está usted muy bonita."* ('Hey! You're very beautiful.') The señoritas giggle girlishly in response. (Where are those fans when you need them?) People are less friendly and accessible at **Amadís**, though both the club and its clientele are more gaudily decked out. The orchestra plays wedding reception versions of standards from the twenties to the nineties. The twirling couples at **Golden Gran Vía** are sedate bordering on arthritic, but this is the closest thing to an actual disco for the more mature set. The decor is much more contemporary than that of most dance halls, with surprisingly uncomfortable brass chairs, fashionably cracked mirrors, and wide screens that screen music videos

THE CLUB SCENE ⟨ THE LOWDOWN

when the live orchestra isn't playing oldies but goodies (i.e., Benny Goodman to Marvin Gaye) for the over-forty set. The constantly changing revues emphasize flash over flesh. In contrast, **Pasapoga** is the kind of endearingly tatty place you'd take your Aunt Esther to after sousing her up on sherry. Even the neon sign outside screams tacky in a thoroughly un-self-conscious way.

Disco dancing... Madrid doesn't really have many discotheques in the American sense of the word, but its examples of the genre rival any in Europe (if not the States) for sheer glitz and glamour. **Angels of Xenon** certainly provides exuberance, thanks to its Felliniesque fashion parade. **Aqualung** is an ultra-weird, wacky disco: one side holds several swimming pools, the other, divided by a monumental glass wall, the dance floor and concert area. Laser lights and disco balls illuminate the fashion victims at **Pachá**, a trendy mélange of drag queens in stilettos and silver mesh and well-bred boys in loafers and dinner jackets. The Top 40 music—ranging from salsa to oldies—is beside the point. **Joy Eslava** is Madrid's most traditional disco, from its luxe 19th-century-theme decor to its endless (by Madrid standards) sardine-packed dance floor swept with the most impressive laser and neon lighting in town. **Palacio de Gaviria** doesn't quite qualify as a classic disco since it's divided into several lovely intimate rooms, each with its own personality, music, and design. Still, it's the second most popular big dance club (after Pachá) with *la gente guapa*. Its real beauty lies in its lack of attitude— the door policy is so liberal that even whale-bellied, tonsorially challenged, Levi-clad tourists shackled in gold chains can enter. Seven stories of nuttiness make **Teatro Kapital** the World Trade Center of discos (predictably, the main dance floor is also the city's largest). If you're over 30 you may feel wildly out of place (and might be stopped politely at the door), but don't let that stop you from going. The ground floor contains the main stage and several bars, but part of the fun is exploring the club's many levels and moods. **Cleofás** caters to a formerly swinging singles crowd trying to shed its fuddy-duddy image by dancing energetically to seventies pop. Aside from the mirrored ceilings, the entrance resembles the living room of your eccentric rich uncle's fifties ranch house.

The Club Scene: Index

Al Andalus. One of the better salas rocieras, with a knowledge-able, excitable crowd... *Tel 556–14–39. Capitán Haya, 19; Cuzco metro stop. Closed Sun.* **(see p. 27)**

Al Lab'Oratorio. Top venue for up-and-coming rock bands, in a variety of indie styles and stylings... *Tel 532–26–69. Colón, 14; Tribunal metro stop. Closes at 3am.* **(see p. 32)**

Amadís. Gussied-up dance hall with dressy but suburban-looking clientele... *Tel 446–00–36; Covarrubias, 42; Bilbao metro stop.* **(see pp. 27, 30, 35)**

Angels of Xenon. The drag shows at this mostly gay disco are legendary; the crowd the town's most eclectic... *Tel 369–38–81; Atocha, 38; Antón Martín metro stop.* **(see pp. 30, 36)**

Aqualung Madrid. An Olympic-size pool, swimming "canals," a fine stage showcasing major players, several bars and dance floors... *Tel 526–59–04. Paseo de la Ermita del Santo, 40 a 48; Puerta de Toledo metro stop. Fri, Sat only.* **(see p. 34)**

Bali Hai. Ramshackle club with cheesy, "tiki"-tacky decor attracts hip club kids and yuppies trying oh so hard.... *Flor Alta, 8; Plaza de España metro stop. Closed Mon–Wed.* **(see p. 26)**

Bocaccio. A young, hip, stand-and-pose crowd patronizes this lavishly decorated after-hours dance club... *Tel 419–19–08. Marqués de la Ensenada, 16; Colón metro stop. Closed Mon, Tue.* **(see pp. 30, 32)**

But. Fancy club for disco or ballroom dancing, luring an upscale clientele... *Tel 448–06–98. Barceló, 11; Tribunal or Bilbao metro stop.* **(see p. 33)**

Café Central. Easily the most elegant, if faded, of the jazz clubs, with top names on the bill... *Tel 369–41–43. Plaza del Ángel, 10; Sol or Antón Martín metro stop.* **(see p. 29)**

Café de Chinitas. The tourist's idea of flamenco, with highly respected José Ortega as featured artist... *Tel 559–51–35. Torija, 7; Santo Domingo metro stop. Closed Sun.*
(see p. 27)

Café del Foro. Serves up a varied menu of sizzling Latino music. The special evenings devoted to magic and comedy are, well, laughable... *Tel 445–37–52. San Andrés, 38; Bilbao metro stop.* **(see p. 32)**

Café del Mercado. Out-of-the-way club specializing in Latino rhythms... *Tel 365–87–39. Ronda de Toledo, 1; Puerta de Toledo metro stop. Open Thur–Sun 11pm–5am.* **(see p. 32)**

Canciller. Nirvana for the grunge set, with a huge following for its live heavy metal/trash concerts... *Tel 306–53–06. Pobladura del Valle, 21; San Blas metro stop. Open Thur 7–11:30pm; Fri, Sat 7pm–5:30am.* **(see p. 29)**

Casa Patas. Elegant ambience and passionate music at this tablao flamenco also known for its tapas, which lure a separate crowd earlier in the evening... *Tel 369–04–96. Cañizares, 10; Antón Martín metro stop.* **(see p. 27)**

Chaquetón. A smoky, sardine-packed, smelly, joyous box where dancers stomp the floor with almost primal abandon... *Tel 671–27–77. Canarias, 39; Palos de la Frontera metro stop. Fridays only.* **(see p. 28)**

Clamores. Madrid's largest jazz venue also hosts an eclectic range of acts, including acoustic pop, folk, blues, soca, and merengue... *Tel 445–79–38. Albuquerque, 14; Bilbao metro stop.* **(see p. 29)**

Cleofás. Clientele at this 40-something disco is solidly local and middle- to upper-middle class... *Tel 576–45–23. Goya, 7; Colón metro. Closed Mon; on Sun, only an early-evening session.* **(see pp. 35, 36)**

Corral de la Morería. This large ritzy space puts on a touristy but invariably excellent flamenco show... *Tel 365–84–46. Morería, 17; Ópera or La Latina metro stop.* **(see p. 27)**

Down. An after-hours clubs, Down doesn't even begin to fill up until around 8am. Claustrophobic on weekends... *Tel 447–04–09. Minas, 20; Noviciado metro stop.* **(see p. 33)**

Empire. Jacket-and-tie is the regular uniform for the snooty 20- and 30-somethings. The music is fairly ordinary.... *Tel 431–54–27. Paseo de Recoletos, 16; Colón or Banco de España metro stop.* **(see pp. 26, 29)**

Goa. Hosts dramatically varied evenings and crowds, though there's usually a gay/lesbian bias, especially during Sunday's wild Shangay Tea Dance, which attracts the entire rainbow spectrum... *Tel 531–48–27. Mesoneros Romanos, 13; Callao metro stop. Closed Mon, Tue.* **(see pp. 30, 33)**

Golden Gran Vía. This dance hall for the more mature set is most crowded just after dinner, when the live orchestra plays between a variety of revues... *Tel 547–11–30. Gran Vía, 54; Callao metro stop.* **(see p. 35)**

Heaven. The mixed gay/straight crowd is as eclectic as the space itself, which veers from futuristic to fusty Edwardian... *Tel 548–20–22. Veneras, 2; Santo Domingo or Sol metro stop. Fri, Sat, after hours only.* **(see p. 33)**

Honky Tonk. Slick homage to American roots music, with clique-ish clientele to match... *Tel 445–68–86. Covarrubias, 24; Alonso Martínez metro stop.* **(see p. 34)**

Joy Eslava. This elaborate disco is Tourist City, with especially-loud Americans, Brits, and Germans. Has a rep among locals as a place for easy pick-ups... *Tel 366–37–33. Arenal, 11; Sol or Opera metro stop.* **(see pp. 26, 35, 36)**

Kabul. Strip off the chrome and neon and you find a genuine throwback to a more fetishist time.... *No phone. Cuesta de Santo Domingo, 1; Santo Domingo metro stop.* **(see p. 31)**

Kathmandu. Madrid's hippest alternative disco, and a dizzy psychedelic experience.... *Tel 541–52–53. Señores de Luzón, 3; Sol metro stop. Closed Sun–Wed.* **(see p. 28)**

Maravillas. Temple of indie rock, with a hip, knowledgeable crowd, including DJs from other clubs... Tel 521–98–80. *San Vicente Ferrer, 35; Tribunal metro stop.*

(see pp. 28, 31)

Midnight. There's surprisingly little attitude here, even at the ultra-hip Thursday night Nature party.... Tel 547–25–25. *Amaniel, 13; Noviciado metro stop. Closed Mon–Wed.* **(see p. 28)**

Morocco. Kitschy "nueva"-movida hangout popular for the Thursday-night house and hip-hop party billed as the House of Devotions... Tel 531–31–77. *Marqués de Leganés, 7; Santo Domingo metro stop. Closed Mon.* **(see p. 26)**

Nature. See Midnight.

Pachá. Madrid's hottest disco, with the most rigorous door policy... Tel 447–01–28. *Barceló, 11; Tribunal metro stop. Closed Sun–Tue.* **(see pp. 30, 33, 36)**

Palace. Thirties-style dance hall attracting a seemingly divorced and desperate crowd... Tel 541–82–30. *Plaza Isabel II, 7; Ópera metro stop.* **(see p. 33)**

Palacio de Gaviria. The palace of posh, though thankfully not of poseurs: 12 exquisite rooms, each devoted to different musical styles, from Latin to ballroom to rock to jazz to swing to techno to reggae... Tel 526–60–69. *Arenal, 9; Ópera or Sol metro stop.* **(see pp. 35, 36)**

Pasapoga. Glitzy old-time dance hall for an older crowd.... Tel 521–50–27. *Gran Vía, 37; Callao metro stop. Closed Mon.* **(see pp. 34, 36)**

Populart. Popular jazz club right smack in the middle of the tourist scene on Calle Huertas... Tel 429–84–07. *Huertas, 22; Antón Martín metro stop.* **(see p. 29)**

El Refugio. Despite this gay disco's chic ancient-Roman-orgy dungeon look, you needn't worry: there are no manacles or shackles in sight.... Tel 369–40–38. *Doctor Cortezo, 1; Sol or Tirso de Molina metro stop. Closed Mon.* **(see p. 31)**

La Rosa. The leading lesbian disco in Madrid, La Rosa specializes in theme nights (the flamenco fest is surprisingly good).... *No phone. Tetuán, 27; Sol metro stop.* **(see p. 30)**

Shangay Tea Dance. See Goa.

Siroco. Soul and funk spin on weekends, but locals jam Siroco for its jamming new bands... *Tel 593–30–70. San Dímas, 3; San Bernardo metro stop. Closed Sun, Mon.* **(see pp. 31, 34)**

El Sol. This mid-sized space with great acoustics and sight lines is primo for top national and occasional international acts... *Tel 532–64–90. Jardines, 3; Sol or Gran Vía metro stop. Closed Sun, Mon.* **(see p. 32)**

La Soleá. Anyone can grab the stage at this lighthearted *sala rociera*... *Tel 365–33–08. Cava Baja, 27; La Latina metro stop.* **(see p. 28)**

Stella. Tourists will love it for one reason alone: the dance floor is a series of galleries overlooking a genuine bowling alley with four lanes... *Tel 522–41–26; Arlabán, 7; Sevilla metro stop. Closed Sun, Mon.* **(see p. 34)**

Strong Center. Don't let the vast dance floor, bars, and pool and foosball tables fool you: this is a gay sex club masquerading as a disco... *Tel 532–15–24; Trujillo, 7; Santo Domingo metro stop.* **(see p. 31)**

Suristán. An exciting eclectic mix of performers play this spacious and handsome club with superb acoustics... *Tel 532–39–09. La Cruz, 7; Sol or Sevilla metro stop. Closed Sun, Mon.* **(see p. 32)**

Swing. The central dance floor at this no-longer-hip bastion of la movida is one of the largest outside an actual disco... *Tel 531–31–13. San Vicente Ferrer, 23; Tribunal metro stop. Closed Sun, Mon.* **(see p. 35)**

Teatro Kapital. A cavernous seven-story space full of dance floors, bars, and theme rooms... *Tel 420–29–06. Atocha, 125; Atocha metro stop. Closed Mon. Open early evening Thur–Sun, late night Tues–Sat.* **(see pp. 34, 36)**

THE CLUB SCENE INDEX

the bar scene

2

It's 4am on a sultry summer morning on the Paseo de la Castellana, a broad, stately boulevard bisected by islands of greenery. Each island contains at least one *terraza* (open-air bar) percolating with debate, perhaps even tinged with eroticism. A matron impeccably turned out in Chanel walks her equally well-manicured poodle and collides with a drag queen mummified in cellophane and lamé, made up in fine contempt for the beautician's art. The two kiss one another on the cheek and move on. A three-generation family, led by an imperious grandmother in a black mantilla commandeers a table, oblivious to the sword-swallowers, fire-eaters, guitarists, and fortune tellers swirling about. At the next table the young man's profile seems unfinished, a quick pen-and-ink caricature of angles and slashes. His long thin fingers and cigarette are like an inverted question mark about to take flight. Agitated yet *intime,* he punctuates his points with little jabs. His companion, as soft and rounded as he is sharp and spare, takes the offensive with a volley of her own. They argue animatedly in that inimitably madrileño way, gesticulating wildly, wielding their cigarettes like demented sushi chefs. Who knows—they could be discussing bombs, or bonds. A pause, and they rise and execute a neat pasodoble around the table. No one takes notice. This is Madrid at night, with its air of genteel anarchy and perpetual paradox....

No wonder John Dos Passos observed in the Roaring Twenties that bars were "the brains and spinal column of Madrid as the Stock Exchange is the central nervous system of New York." Little has changed as the city roars into a new millennium, except perhaps that bars now function as Madrid's lifeblood as well.

There are more than 18,000 bars in central Madrid, a total that—conservatively—exceeds that in all of Scandinavia. They go by various names (there are almost as many as there are Eskimo words for snow), and the distinctions are often blurry. *Mesones, tabernas, tascas taperías* (tapas bars), *cafés, bares, disco-bares, cervecerías* (beer saloons), *sidrerías* (cider houses), *cocktelerías, whiskerías, champagnerías,* even *chocolaterías,* whatever their specialty, all serve a full array of booze—and coffee—throughout the night. So don't assume anything called a *café* is necessarily the local equivalent of a Starbucks; it's not.

Since nearly every establishment in Madrid qualifies as a bar, refer also to Late Night Dining, Hanging Out, and The Club Scene for further recommendations. And feel free to wander, following the crowd and your instincts. The streets listed below under "The Beaten Path" all pulsate and pullulate well into the night; there can be as many as ten bars in a single block, as clogged at 4am as a New York City subway car at rush hour, particularly on Friday and Saturday.

Tapas, *Tertulias*, and *Terrazas*

Along with the three Ms (*la movida, la marcha,* and *la madrugada,* see What's Hot, What's Not), the three Ts—*tapas, tertulias,* and *terrazas*—explain the basics of Madrid nightlife. Tapas are nibbles—anything from a simple plate of olives to octopus in garlic sauce, meant to tide you over between 6 and 10pm, before dinner. *Tapa* means lid and refers to an old Andalusian custom of serving a snack on a small plate that could be used to prevent dust, ashes, and/or flies from settling in your glass of wine. Ritual dictates that you order one or two selections per bar, while making the rounds; it's not uncommon to hit five or more tapas bars in one evening (you'll find several clustered within a small area). Tapas are served in three portions: *pincho* (a bite), *tapa* (a small serving), or *ración* (practically appetizer-size); all prices are listed at the bar, and you pay after eating (how the waiters juggle the plates and keep the tabs straight is a mystery). If you sit at a table there's usually a 25-percent surcharge. Most bars offer tapas in the 400–1,500 ptas. range, depending on the ingredients and complexity of preparation. It's considered impolite to point, but if you don't *habla,* do it anyway, tossing in a casual *"Eso, por favor!"* (that, please). And don't worry about yelling to make yourself heard; everyone else does.

Which brings us to another beloved Madrid tradition, the *tertulia,* loosely defined as any social gathering for purposes of discussion—heated debate, really—of a specific topic, usually politics, philosophy, or the arts. The custom dates back to the Enlightenment; at night the cafes noted for their *tertulias* seem to simmer with incipient rebellion. Some virtually become ongoing salons, attracting literati, glitterati, and assorted hangers-on, clinging like remoras hoping for scraps. Certain bars post tertulia topics for the week; other tertulias are far less structured, spreading like brush fires as sparks of pure reason and cigarette cinders illuminate a dim corner.

Terrazas are essentially al fresco cafes; most are located along major boulevards, squares, and parks. Some are outdoor extensions of indoor cafes, others makeshift shells (*kioskos*) that come alive at night. The focal point of socializing in the summer, a popular *terraza* can serve as a combination restaurant/bar/disco/concert venue. They're as ubiquitous as stateside hot-dog stands, though they're less dependable, vulnerable as they are to Madrid's fickle finger of fashion. The hippest hug the paseos of Recoletos and Castellana. A younger, poorer crowd lines the Pintor de Rosales and Bailén at the edge of the Parque del Oeste and Casa de Campo, or the patio of the 1720 barracks known as Cuartel Conde Duque. But *terrazas* can and do spring up virtually anywhere there's an open space.

The Beaten Path

Madrid's nightlife is mostly focused in several barrios, each of which has its own distinct personality and ambience. All are located within a couple of miles of each other in the compact city center. The **Argüelles/Moncloa** area holds the University and several student-frequented bars, but the young and restless usually move east to Bilbao and Malasaña as the night progresses. **Malasaña** starts at the Plaza Dos De Mayo, famed as the sight of a peasant uprising against Napoleon's troops in 1808. The area has retained something of that revolutionary spirit. The hub of progressive "indie" rock clubs and bars, it's frankly known for drugs and dregs, the sweet scents of garlic and ganja commingling in the night air. Those who can't afford to drink in a bar buy a liter of beer at a grocery and hang out in the streets. **Fuencarral** marks Malasaña's unofficial eastern border; La Palma, San Vicente Ferrer, San Andrés, and San Pablo are the streets to stroll. Just to the north, Bilbao (especially the streets of San Bernardo, Hartzenbusch, Alburquerque, Cardenal Cisneros, and Palafox) has been getting the spillover from Malasaña, and a cleaner-cut sort of crowd. **Plaza Mayor/Plaza Santa Ana** (and surrounding picturesque winding alleys like Cuchilleros) comprise the most touristy section of Madrid. Adjacent to this area are several of the best streets for tapas (try Echegaray) and music (especially Huertas, good for everything from classical to karaoke); youthful foreigners and the madrileños who love them prowl these streets with the intensity of caged lions. On nearby drags like **Moratín**, the folk seem so young they practically qualify as street urchins, and the air reeks with gas fumes from dozens of

INTRODUCTION ⟋ THE BAR SCENE

motorbikes. **Salamanca** is a more upscale, residential neighborhood; the fancy boutiques along its avenues display designer labels. Lagasca, Serrano, Velázquez, and Juan Bravo streets are the province of the pijos—the snooty and wealthy. Just southeast of Malasaña, off of Gran Vía, is **Chueca,** the gay ghetto. Here you'll find two dozen mostly seedy bars crammed into a five-square block area. Southeast of Plaza Mayor, **Lavapiés** has become home to many hip, alternative bars, where the more radical gay/lesbian element hangs (check out Calle Torrecilla del Leal). This neighborhood merges in the west with **La Latina,** another traditionally working class district, now bustling with lower-key (straight) bars catering to the artier 20- and 30-somethings. Cava Baja and Segovia are two of the better-known bar-hopping streets.

Timing is Everything

Cafés, tascas, mesones, cervecerías, and *tabernas* are frequented after work and during tapas time. After dinner (around midnight) it's time to *ir de copas* (literally, go out for drinks—in a hard-core way). This could be at either a *cocktelería* or *bar de copas.* Or you could find a hole in the wall for music *en vivo* (live), then dance at a disco-bar until discoteca time (around 3–4am). True night owls will repair to a *chocolatería* or *churrería* (named after the fried donuts called *churros*) for a quick pick-me-up around 6 or 7am, before moving on to an afterhours club.

Etiquette

Even alcoholic intake follows a pattern, increasing in volume and proof as the night progresses. Just after work and during tapas-time, *cerveza* (beer, usually ordered in a *caña,* or ¼-liter glass), *vino* (a *chato* is a small glass, a *vaso* slightly larger), *sidra* (hard cider), and *fino* and *manzanilla* (types of sherry) are the beverages of choice. Dinner is accompanied by a bottle of wine. With plenty of food in the system (madrileños carefully regulate their drinking to their eating), post-midnight is the true cocktail hour, with martinis and single malts currently enjoying the same vogue they are stateside. But you'll rarely see a falling-down local drunk. Spaniards possess an innate sense of pride and dignity, and inebriation is considered indecorous. That being said, however, Madrid is so permissive it makes even Amsterdam and

Copenhagen seem puritanical, this despite (or perhaps because of?) Spain's stout and devout brand of Catholicism. While cocaine remains fairly easy to get, the drugs of choice, especially among Gen-X types, are X (Ecstasy) and Special K (ketamine). And no matter what designer drug is in vogue, walk into almost any club or disco-bar in the hipper-than-thou Malasaña and Bilbao neighborhoods, and the aroma of hash smacks you in the face.

Bars in Central Madrid

Alhama **9**
Alkalde **71**
Almendro 13 **16**
El Anciano Rey
  de los Vinos **42**
La Ardosa **87**
Asquiniña **17**
Bagatelle **69**
El Balcón de
  Rosales **1**
Bar César Ritz **25**
Bar Cock **48**
Bar Taurino **30**
Berlín Cabaret **14**
Black and White **64**
Bocaíto **51**
Bodega de Roberto
  el Pirata **66**
Bolero **79**
Las Bravas **40**
El Brillante **23**
Café Acuerela **61**
Café Comercial **93**
Café Figueroa **59**
Café Galdós **58**
Café Gijón **67**
Café Manuela **89**
Café La Troje **62**
Calentito **7**
Candela **19**
Candilajas **13**
Capote **83**
Cardenal **94**
Casa Labra **43**
Cervercería
  Alamena **31**
Chicote **46**
La Ciberteca **81**
Círculo de Ballas
  Artes **45**
Cruising **57**
Las Cuevas del
  Sésamo **33**
Del Diego **49**
Errota-Zar **44**
El Espejo **68**
Fabrica del Pan **55**
Los Gabrieles **36**
Los Gatos **24**
Gayarre **80**
La Gloria **10**
The Irish Rover **77**
Houston's Cattle Company **5**
Isis **65**
José Luis **74**
Kairós **15**
Kamelot **95**
King Creole **88**
Kingston's **70**

Lerranz **27**
Lhardy **38**
Libertad 8 **52**
Louie Louie **91**
La Lupe **21**
La Madriguera **12**
Matador **29**
Mito **63**
Moby Dick **76**
El Mojito **20**
El Mollete **6**
El Moskito **22**
Museo del Jamón **39**
Nell's **75**
Net Café **2**
No Fun **90**
Oba-Oba **8**
Old Fox Tavern **82**
Paláez **73**
Rick's **50**
La Riviera **11**
La Rotonda **26**
El Salón del Prado **28**
San Mateo Seis **85**
Stars Café-Dance **47**
Taberno de
  Antonio Sánchez **18**
La Tapería **3**
Tatoom Road **78**
Teatriz **72**
Top XI **56**
Torero **41**
Torito **54**
La Trucha **34**
Truco **60**
Tupperware **86**
Vaivén **84**
La Venencia **37**
La Vía Lactea **92**
Villa Rosa **32**
Viva Madrid **35**
Why Not? **53**
Zúkero **4**

Church	†
Information	ⓘ
Metro	Ⓜ
Post Office	⊠

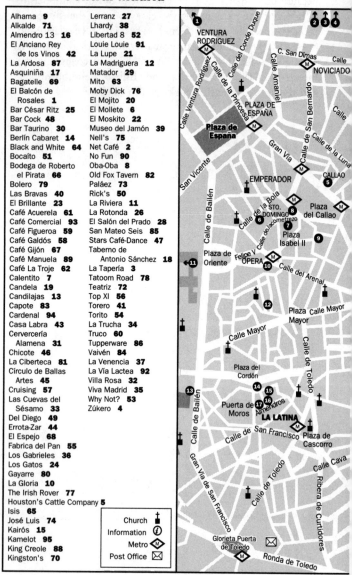

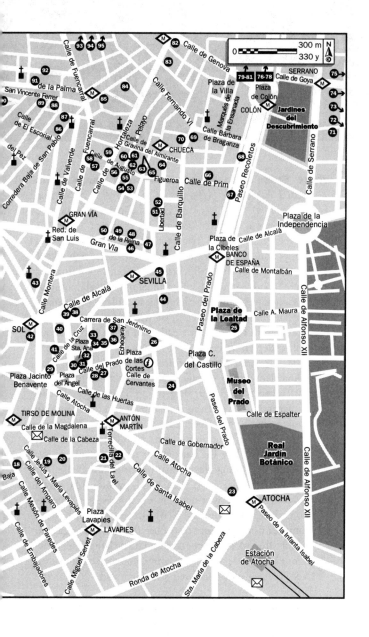

The Lowdown

Where Spain's most famous director hangs out...
Pedro Almodóvar (*Women on the Verge of a Nervous Breakdown*) and his cronies patronize **La Gloria**, and might just as well have designed it as their own private playpen/film set. The style is established at the entrance: a "shop" window with a black-and-white chair lying askew, matching high-heel slippers, and a bottle spilling red stage blood. Mondrian and Buñuel might well have collaborated on the interior: huge quasi-cubist mosaics making an almost surreal contrast with enormous candles which seem stolen from a cathedral and a neo-Baroque ceiling depicting the devil consorting with lesbian angels. Extraterrestrial best describes the throngs, from wan ethereal droids in metallic garb to Terminator cyborgs with muscles bulging in form-fitting Batman gear. **Berlín Cabaret** offers everything from cabaret (oddly enough) to comedy, but it really specializes in drag shows. With two cramped floors, performers can't help but interact with the audience; hug the balcony for the best views of the Amazons teetering precariously on the iron staircase that spirals above the stage. The highly fashionable crowd buzzes about like hyperactive mosquitoes; sexual orientation is beside the point. At **El Mojito**, dig the gay Kens in compromising positions by the bar, then shift your gaze to admire the colorful paper crab and turtle lampshades, the hannered bronze sun, fringe lamps, and the stylish, 'tude-free gay/lesbian/bi/confused/straight crowd.

Barred at the door... **Nell's** is a classic see-and-be-seen hangout, a favored haunt of the royal family. You half expect to pass through a metal detector, or to get thoroughly frisked by the humorless doormen. A soda alone will set you back 1,250 ptas. ($10)—helps keep the riffraff out. At the so hot/so cool **Bar Cock** the desirable center tables are booked for VIPs; while you stand, those tables sit empty, waiting for someone famous (or an entourage) to enter. And some toupeed bigwig, from a producer to the artist of the moment, invariably does. The main floor screams exclusivity: antique marble fireplace, beveled glass, terra-cotta floors, beamed ceilings, and dark wood paneling. The downstairs is sexier and more outrageous, with jello colors, gold leafing, and the ultimate testament to testosterone: posters, drawings, etchings, cartoons, and gouaches of roosters in full crow (an apt description of the crowd, regardless of gender). The name **Torero** suits, if only because when you arrive you'll feel like a matador confronting the bull (in the guise of burly bouncers at the door). This is the kind of place where everyone thinks they belong in *People's* 100 Most Beautiful People issue. Downstairs they shed their jackets and inhibitions and dance like computer nerds to a nonstop beat that pulses from techno to Top 40.

Wacky watering holes... A mosaic from heavy metal rockers to off-duty drag queens patronizes tiny **Torito** late nights. They match the equally unpredictable decor, which features a twisted collage of cuttings on the blood-red walls that looks like it might have been created by a photo editor who enjoyed decapitating Barbie dolls as a kid. Add disco balls, multi-hued lightbulbs, and potent cocktails, and it's no surprise the room starts spinning rapidly. The tone at **Why Not?** is set by the lifesize cutout of Marilyn Monroe, stills of movie icons from Dietrich to Dean, and a tatty, trembling crystal bead chandelier that looks like a reject from a bus-and-truck tour of *Phantom.* You'll also hear the best dish in town among the mixed gay and straight and Madrid's chattiest, cattiest waiters. **Matador** is all middle-neo-high Clutter, incorporating parodies of Goya's fleshy *Naked Maja,* huge mannequins, *porrones* (ceramic wine jugs), rusting hardware (from innocent pails to dungeonesque chains), and ropes everywhere (you half expect the athletic, ponytailed, hoop-earringed bartenders to swing from them). **Calentito** sports mobiles of celestial bodies (dangling dangerously close to dancers), painted glass balls, model airplanes, and illuminated plastic minotaurs in blinding colors. You feel almost voyeuristic watching the slithery crowd and the drag princesses still in the morphing stage—ectomorphic, futuristic, luminescent, hermaphroditic—slinking about in bodysuits that show lots of (unstrategic) flesh while negotiating narrow ledges set with smoldering tapers. **Star's Café-Dance** is zanily decorated with ocher walls, scrap-metal sculptures (quite possibly fashioned by artist/customers running a tab), abstract paintings, figurative tapestries, marble floors, surprisingly tasteful cherubim, and campily cheesy crescent moons dangling drunkenly from the ceiling. Even the bathrooms are cool, with sheer glass vanities on steel ball-bearing bases, tile floors. The crowd veers dramatically hour by hour, from poor grad students to patrician bankers, roughshod bikers to spike-heeled drag princesses. **Bodega de Roberto el Pirata** is wild and witty, with whacked-out abstract erotic paintings (the turquoise walls serve as a rotating gallery), most in Fauvist colors matching the clientele's hair, painted metal bird lamps, piñatas, exposed pipes, and a remarkable papier-mâché mermaid with fangs. **Capote** is so hip even off-duty bartenders come here to drink. It's obnoxiously retro-chic: zinc bar, blue Plexiglass, and maroon Naugahyde seats. The spaced-out crowd tends to be clean-cut but still cutting-edge. Those who only wear black (including scowls) should adore the genuine Gypsy hangout **Candela**. It doesn't even begin to hop until 3am, when all the top flamenco artists end up here, often giving an impromptu gig, and really letting their cascading hair down, in the grotty grotto downstairs. Most of the men sport greasy ponytails, huge moustaches, garish gold jewelry, and glowering glares, while several women don't seem to have bathed in days. But consider yourself lucky indeed if you're "invited" downstairs for a performance. If you're not, you can enjoy the amusing spectacle of what Gypsies call "white" yuppie pretenders doing a stomp around a few tables upstairs. The Gypsies tolerate them: after all, they're paying (and round-buying) customers.

Historic haunts... The immortal celeb hangout **Chicote**, which opened in 1931, is so revered that not even the Civil War could close it down for a night. It seems caught in a fifties time warp: seasick-green Naugahyde banquettes, smaller jade booths for discreet encounters, fake plastic oak paneling; the only modernization in 40 years has been the track lighting. After a down-at-its-high-heels period when it gained notoriety as a high-class hooker bar, Chicote got a new lease on life post Franco. Today its reputation for knockout concoctions and aura of fairy-tale elegance keep it packed with tourists and fashionable locals alike. **Café Comercial** looks little changed since Socialists, intellectuals, and artists made the place seethe with debate in the twenties and thirties. You're sure to see shrunken, withered men in traditional black berets huddled in a corner, playing dominoes and reminiscing in querulous voices about the good old days. The striking decor might best be described as functional fin de siècle: marble, mirrors, chandeliers, leather banquettes, and a zinc-backed bar. **Café Gijón** is another mythic Madrid tradition, where everyone who's anyone has made a pit stop since 1888. Essentially the Madrid version of New York's famed Elaine's, Gijón is a surprisingly dowdy meet-and-greet spot for literati and glitterati, who preach at the long oak bar and preen in the gilt mirrors. The tapas are pricey and basic but expertly prepared (favorite choices include the marinated anchovies, veal sausage, and artichokes). Pablo Iglesias founded the Socialist Party at **Casa Labra** in 1879, perhaps as a reaction to the room's ornate flourishes—zinc-topped bar, magnificent gilt mirrors, and delicate tracery painted on the walls. *Tertulias* continue to hail like sniper bullets over the tapas (stick to croquetas, chorizo, cheeses, and cod—especially the lip-smacking, batter-fried salt cod strips, *soldaditos*).

Painting the town pink... **Rick's** is the Ritz of gay bars. *Everybody Comes to Rick's* was the play on which *Casablanca* was based, and the name fits: Every gay night crawler strolls in at some point in the evening. The comparatively lavish decor includes the requisite Bogie paraphernalia, gilt columns, marble floors, and huge gold-plated dishes; tented fabrics and arches give the bar itself a Moorish feel. A total contrast is provided by the equally popular, aptly named **Cruising**, where younger guys break in their new leather jackets, and the rough trade likes to break in new arrivals. Most of the fellows here have one-track minds—and they're unlikely to be derailed. Seedy? Sure, but therein lies its considerable appeal. The claustrophobic upstairs bar at **Mito** is notable for its vivid aqua hue and a wall egotistically devoted to photos of the sexy young owner hugging half of Madrid. The downstairs is roomier, but not from 10:30pm on, when local fave Joaquin Jurado performs his drag set for everyone from graying distinguished exec types to unabashed diesel dykes. The name, **Black and White** (aka Blanco y Negro), refers more to the decor than the clientele (although you'll notice a stark contrast among the patrons as well: young Lotharios on the make and the older men who want to make them). It's the king of gay striptease and queen of drag shows. **Isis** is the lesbian bar currently in vogue; its decor, while vaguely exotic (flaming torches, Japanese lanterns) hardly recalls the Egyptian goddess of fertility. Late weekend evenings it's mobbed by women with spiked blond hair or blacker-than-black Louise Brooks bangs, along with a few of their more flamboyant (or would that be "flamgirlant"?) male friends. **Top XI** is best known for its happy hour, which lures a slightly older crowd and packs the place around 11. The music, while top-notch, is so loud you can't hear the person standing next to you. The seedy decor favors porn postcards, and the psychedelic strobe lights could give even non-epileptics a fit if they stare too hard. It's nominally a lesbian bar, but everyone ends up at **Truco** throughout the week. The electric blue Spartan box becomes one teeming dance floor by 2am with everyone writhing about, predictably to k.d. Lang, Melissa Etheridge, and Madonna.

Gay and lesbian alternatives... You can get looped at **La Lupe** (the drinks are strong indeed), but it's definitely not a pick-up place, just a casual spot for gays and lesbians to intermingle and discuss everything from political agendas to real- and reel-life soap operas. It boasts a high percentage of pretty-boy fashion victims, albeit the kind who sew pink triangles into their denim jackets. The decor is equally stylish, with mango walls offset by exposed midnight-blue pipes. Gays and lesbians flock to the wittily decorated Lavapiés bar, **El Mojito**, to escape Chueca attitude and sexcapades and savor the eponymous Cuban cocktail (knockout combos of rum, lemon, and mint). Just around the corner, **El Moskito** has softer light and harder-edged music than the others. The atmosphere is more intense and politicized: Posters for all the gay/lesbian community centers obscure the fashionable blood-orange and crimson walls. The mood is lighter in the room at the rear, fittingly painted sunshine yellow.

Pink cafe society... Café **Figueroa** is a relaxed place where gays can sip a *cerveza* without fear of being hit upon. The crowd ranges from cool East Village–style nerds (buzz cuts, leather sneakers, gold granny glasses) to dignified 40-something businessmen still in their suits. The space is very attractive, with etched-glass doors, lace curtains, Oriental carpets, wrought-iron and marble tables, 1930s radios, even wicker peacock chairs (which contrast nicely with the pool table). The classically camp yet comfortable **Café Acuarela** resembles a United Nations garage sale reinvented by an imaginative decorator: Victorian gilt-and-velour love seats, Balinese masks, Indian tapestries, sinuous candlesticks, a jungle of potted plants, and big, plater-of-paris angels in uncertain taste. At the laid-back **Café La Troje**, the ongoing *tertulia* is between bartenders and customers over the choice of CDs (the waitstaff is both animated and adorable). And the decor is quite comely, with old clocks, chandeliers, mustard walls, black-and-white photos, and a marble-top bar. **Café Galdós** is a faded turn-of-the-century place with worn woodwork, lace curtains, and smoked glass. It's a popular early-evening gathering spot for the genteel, aging gay and lesbian crowd, from men flaunting their graying temples to women with lacquered hair and too much eyeliner. Everyone is affable, only occasionally playing peekaboo from above their newspapers. The inimitable **La Madriguera**, a combination bookstore/gallery/cafe, is owned by lesbians, but everyone's welcome. The regulars reflect its liberal policy—everyone from stylish women execs trailing Chanel in their wake to unkempt intellectual sorts whose credo might be "I stink, therefore I am."

Besotted by the old sod... Though it's just a dusty square room with a few casks and barrels (and wildly clashing Goya and Guinness posters), **La Ardosa** is credited with starting the Irish pub boom, simply by offering Guinness on tap in the eighties. In contrast, the **Irish Rover** is throughly yupster. The duplex space duplicates not only a classic Dublin pub, but a classic Dublin street corner as well: faux-brick exterior and Victorian gas street lamps inside complement the polished wood paneling and bar, elegant stairwell, and stone floors. Can busts of Joyce and Yeats be far behind? **Old Fox Tavern** offers a wide array of beers and spirits, in addition to the best Irish rock bands on weekends. U2 will appreciate the Guinness posters and electronic darts. It attracts a mix of Brit expats and local youths who look like they'd prefer rugby to soccer; the wide-screen TV is perpetually turned to Eurosport.

Where to find Spanish yuppies... Just like matadors, the nouveaus at **Torero** stand, pose, and flounce about with a flourish. How fitting that the large, round, mirrored bar permits equal-opportunity primping. Herman Melville might spout off at the hysterically nautical decor at **Moby Dick** (oars, whales, harpoons, fishnets, even submarine-style doors) but the yuppie clientele has a whale of a time. The trendoid professional clientele at **Bagatelle** starts shimmying early—perhaps because they all look like furtive workaholics taking a quick break. **Zúkero** is a prime example of the incomprehensible popularity of many Madrid bars. Upmarket bankers and stock brokers dressed downscale cram this unremarkable gargantuan space. Don't be deterred by doormen at **Vaivén,** even though they look as if they belong in a flick about corrupt boxers. The dressy crowd slums here only because it's the sole Malasaña disco-bar with a real dance floor. Vaivén's DJs spin slightly blunted cutting-edge techno/industrial. The entrance to **Tatoom Road** strikes the right bizarre note for the young pijo crowd: Greco-Roman columns supporting a brick-and-marble triangular lintel flanked by neon beer and ale signs. It's designed to make yuppies feel that they, too, can get as grungy and hi-techno as any club kid. The giant wide-screen TV and several pool tables almost make it fell like a sports bar. The Salamanca location of **José Luis** was the first and remains the best in this chain, which was propelled by a proper, prosperous crowd. The interior is as well manicured as the clientele. The blond wood, mirrors, and pink tablecloths give it a coldly artificial feel.

Rock around the clock... **King Creole** is a shrine to good ol' rockabilly, right down to the guitars, soda fountain artifacts, and posters of the greats, from Chuck Berry to Presley. It's jammed and jamming with a surprisingly youthful crowd; they even look the part, going back to the future with sideburns, pompadours, and beehives. **Louie Louie** displays psychedelic Peter Max–style posters and photos of legends in concert, from the King to the Kinks,

Jerry Lee Lewis to James Brown (which gives you an idea of what the DJs spin). The decor is mostly black with splashes of carnelian (also an apt description of attire here). It has the most American feel of the Malasaña bars, with T-shirts for sale, a pool table in the back room (so small they should supply sawed-off cue sticks), even Fred Flintstone yabba-dabba-doing on the men's room door.

Where to hear local bands... Up-and-coming local grunge and garage rock bands are featured in the dark, jail-like basement of **Bodega de Roberto el Pirata**, where squeezing through to the rest rooms means negotiating a throng that insists on slam-dancing despite the lack of a spare inch. **San Mateo Seis** is perhaps the quintessential (if superficially indistinguishable) Malasaña bar, with black walls, a truly morbid mural of cavorting skeletons, black-clad disaffected grungeniks, and nihilistic lyrics from the up-to-the-minute indie to industrial acts. **La Vía Láctea** means Milky Way. Although the acts may no longer be out-of-this-world, it remains a sentimental favorite as the first of Madrid's heavy rock bars, with two decades' worth of pasted-over posters (even on the ceiling). Throw in music videos, weirdly lit pictures, graffiti, and a punctiliously punkish crowd, and you have a grunge classic. Go upstairs when the music's live: you get a better view and the tables are discreetly spaced so you can almost talk. Rebel yuppies and buzzed, buzz-cut types congregate at **Fábrica de Pan**. The three rooms feature cool, disturbing photos, tattered posters, weird tile work, and abstract primitive paintings plastered against burnt-orange and maroon walls (the same adjectives could describe the bands—which have names like Nine Pound Hammer or Crank + Monkey Nuts—as well as their music).

Tile one on... Nearly every Madrid bar of a certain age boasts absolutely breathtaking tile work. First on everyone's list is **Los Gabrieles**. Don't go for the tapas, but rather to giggle at the gawking tourists. The inventive artistry ranges from the majestic to the macabre, from vibrant bullfighting scenes to equally vivid skeletons. The Cordoba tile floors and black lacquer tables contribute to the urbane ambience (especially amusing considering that its now off-limits cellar was a Gypsy whorehouse for many years). **Viva Madrid** runs a close second, with vaulted beamed ceiling, arches,

THE BAR SCENE ◡ THE LOWDOWN

marvelous murals that resemble daguerreotypes and tile work depicting turn-of-the-century Madrid scenes (typically, the subjects embrace each other passionately), even old nudie postcards. In the fifties, it hosted such larger-than-life celebs as Orson Welles, Louis Armstrong, Ava Gardner, and the great bullfighter Manolete (with whom Gardner allegedly had a torrid affair).

In Hemingway's footsteps... Cervecería Alemana may be a disappointment to Papa-philes: Not one souvenir or sign proclaiming "Hemingway Drank Here" is in evidence. But he did, religiously, before, during, and after the Spanish Civil War. The bar could easily have been plucked straight from a Hemingway short story: a symphony of lovely old blond wood doors, bullfight photos and posters, steins, and brown-and-beige walls. Everyone who's anyone has caroused at **Chicote**, from Hemingway (who reputedly drafted his wartime press dispatches from here) to Ava Gardner, Grace Kelly, Luis Buñuel, and Gary Cooper (whose autographed photos adorn the walls).

Ethnic sounds... The multiethnic spirit at the multilevel **Kingston's** is reflected in the music, the clientele, even the decor: Nigerian batiks, vivid Rasta colors, graffiti, Peruvian paintings. This is the best place to hear soul, funk, reggae, calypso, and ska artists on tour. Don't miss the gallery-quality Caribbean art naif and witty cartoons on race. At **Oba-Oba** a few scraggly palm fronds, unconvincing homemade Carnival masks, phosphorescent colors, and a wall of sugar cane suffice for decor. But, oh my, the *caipirinhas* (sugar-cane liquor and lime drinks) and *mojitos*, the sizzling samba, the half-naked men and women beaded with sweat swarming on the petite dance floor—fan, please! **Calentito** is a luscious, occasionally laughable Latin club, but the music and scene both live up to the name's promise: *muy caliente*, with sultry salsa, merengue, and lambada, and Latino Freds and Gingers blending into one another on the dance floor. The ornate Mudejar **Villa Rosa** doesn't heat up until 1am, when its international just-out-of-school-to-senior-professorial crowd thrust along to throbbing salsa, merengue, and bolero. It's very popular with *guiris* (foreigners) and *la gente guapa* alike.

Down and dirty... More than half the Malasaña bars would qualify, but you can take this category quite literally if you want to discover where the jaded get down in the most unsanitary surroundings. The name **No Fun** is appropriate depending on what hour you arrive. Too early (2–5am) or too late (after 7am), and it's dead. In between, hard and deafening rock and roll animates scrawny, scraggly club zombies who at this point look like dyspeptic chihuahuas. The murals are as leeringly provocative as a Crumb cartoon: bearded women and ravenously toothy male rockers with oversized tongues, all engaged in various sexual acts. The black walls are plastered with posters of indie bands with names like The First Sex Museum and The Pleasant Fuckers. While nose rings are common, it draws its share of hip cleaner-cut types as well. Indeed, everyone looks bad—yet somehow nice. Still, years of scrubbing couldn't erase the rancid odor of hash and sweat. Walk through the black leather curtains at the entryway of **Tupperware** and you step into a Flower Power acid trip: dizzying black-and-white striped walls, neon-hued stencils of nude chicks boogying and generally getting down, rude graffiti, and mismatched fifties-style ranch-house bar stools. The most flattering thing to say about the interior is that the women's john has toilet paper.

For cyberholics... **Net Café** caters to the college set, who net cheap *cervezas* while researching their term papers on-line or chatting with friends overseas. The computer monitors are cunningly embedded in the glass tables to protect them from beer spillage. **La Ciberteca** is the preserve of businesspeople, mostly in their 30s, who appreciate the less wired ambience. It's well lit and stylish, with modern artwork, sleek but uncomfortable metal chairs, mesh electric lamps, even cool T-shirts for sale. PCs, but not Macs, are available at both. Your software may not be compatible, but you can certainly send e-mail, surf, or cyber-chat. Remember the keyboards are in Spanish, meaning keys like "n" with a tilde, but everything else is standard.

What's on tapas? (best eats)... **Bocaíto** lassos a lively set for its sublime, unusual tapas. The horseshoe-shaped bar is lucky indeed for those with more adventuresome palates. Smoked baby eels, lambs' brains, a practically definitive *callos a la madrileña* (tripe in spicy tomato sauce). If you find offal awful, more standard standards include *mojama* (cured, sun-baked, air-dried tuna), *huevos revueltos* (scrambled eggs), and luscious, garlicky grilled prawns. **Lhardy** is a fabulously neo-Baroque restaurant (see Late Night Dining) but madrileños also converge here for the excellent gourmet delicatessen in front, which offers tempting tapas from glittering glass cases and *caldo* (a broth reputed to cure the worst hangover) from a silver-plated samovar. **El Anciano Rey de los Vinos** (The Old King of Wines) provides an excellent selection of wines by the glass. The specialty is the yummy *torrijas*, bread soaked in wine and spices, dusted with sugar, then deep fried. **Lerranz** is snooty, but the tapas are worth the attitude, including perfectly textured *langostinos a la plancha* (leviathan grilled prawns), tender octopus with coarse potatoes in garlic sauce, and the unusual, delectably tart *ensalada mora* (mulberry salad). Connoisseurs appreciate the sterling Andalusian tapas at **La Trucha**, including cod pâté, smoked trout canapés, and eel in garlic sauce. The aged wood casks and peeling posters burnished gold by years of cigarettes indicate the specialty of the dark, cramped **La Venancia**: sherry, sherry, and more sherry. It's all they serve to drink. The tapas may lack imagination, but they're intensely flavored (meant to showcase the sherry, not the other way around): briny marinated olives, the aforementioned *mojama*, blue-cheese canapés. Muted pop and jazz play in the background at the mellow **Errota-Zar** as the solidly professional crowd savors excellent *txacoli* (a flinty white wine from the Basque Country) and such specialties as cod croquettes. The no-frills, no-nonsense Madrid standby, **Las Bravas**, is famed for inventing one of the simplest tapas around, *patatas bravas:* roast potatoes liberally doused with a savory peppery sauce that'd make even a Texan's eyes water. (If the potatoes don't make you blink, the savagely bright neon lighting and zilch decor will.) Recently restored to its original grandeur, the yuppified **Almendro 13** in the working-class La Latina neighborhood offers delicious Castilian tapas like tripe, blood sausage, and sea bream in garlic sauce, as well as a young, hip clientele that looks oddly out of place amid the old-fashioned trappings (brick walls, wood beams, old clocks, and pottery).

Peláez must have ransacked several attics for the ravishing collection of embossed brass plates, hand-painted platters, *porrones* (rough ceramic wine jugs), and brilliantly decorated lances from the King's Guard. It's justly celebrated for its *tortillas* (omelettes), stuffed peppers, canapés (including a delectable partridge), and *ahumados* (house-smoked fish from cod to tuna). At **Alkalde** a yuppie, older crowd lingers in a charmingly rustic setting over sublime seafood tapas like *chipirones en su tinta* (squid in ink) and prawns with mushrooms, and Basque favorites like *chistorra* (sausage laced with paprika). A cool if chilly clientele enjoys the tasty, tasteful tapas at the Philippe Starck–designed **Teatriz**. They're also surprisingly reasonable, if you stick to simpler items like fried chorizos; velvety cheese and prawn croquettes; and cheese steeped in vinegar. **Asquiniña** is little more than a brightly lit hole in the wall but the traditional Galician tapas are positively incandescent. Locals scarf down the *pulpo* (grilled octopus) and *lacon* (corned beef).

What's on tapas? (widest selection)... The upscale **José Luis** resembles an upscale Horn and Hardart's (down to the stolidly continental Eisenhower eats). Try the *canapé de solomillo* (juicy, bite-sized open-faced sirloin sandwiches), smoked salmon tartar, or *ensalada de can-grejo* (chunky crabmeat salad fragrant with garlic, peppers, onion, and cumin). **El Brillante** looks like an automat without the little coin-operated windows for chicken potpie. This is one of the cheapest tapas bars in town; it stays open 24 hours a day so you can satisfy your craving anytime, for anything from *churros* to *chorizo*, burgers to bocadillos. Next to the snazzy etched glass mirrors, the only other significant design element at **Museo del Jamón** is the array of enormous cured hams and chorizos hanging from the ceiling, cheek-by-jowl with the occasional fowl, baguette, or wheel of overripe, aromatic cheese (try the sharp Manchego or tangy blue Cabrales). The yummies at **El Espejo** are surprisingly affordable, given its swank location and reputation. Specialties include veal meatballs, smoked salmon *revueltos* (scrambled eggs with salmon), and peppered pork loin. **La Tapería** is popular with students and struggling 20-somethings because of its inexpensive but savory tapas from around Spain, including salt cod, bull's tail, and various *tortillas* (omelettes).

Cocktail parties... The nickname of **Chicote** is "Museo de Bebidas"—as in a "beverage museum" devoted to the art of the fine cocktail. Don't even try to stump the bartenders, but do try the Cocktail Chicote: gin, Campari, vermouth, Grand Marnier, and Creme de Lima. **Bar Cock** has become the refuge of aging golden boys and silver-haired grandes dames, replete with entourages in tow and under foot; the movers-and-shakers are stirred by the martini-martinet barkeeps, who are scrupulous in preparing their concoctions. Debonair is the operative word at **Del Diego** after dinner, when you can argue the proportions of a pousse-café or discourse on single malts and ports (they have a savvy selection) with the knowledgeable bartender, and relax in a civilized environment. The decor was out even when it was in: sliding glass doors, wood floors, and "living" leather furniture that morphs depending on the occupant's shape and weight. Every evening the bartender at the **Bar César Ritz** earns a new honorary degree in mixology by serving such creations as the Ritz Diana (rum, Benedictine, lime juice) or César Ritz (red vermouth, crème de cacao, egg yolk) to the likes of Naomi Campbell and Dennis Quaid. If beer ain't to your liking, pardner, the barkeeps at **Houston's Cattle Company** can rustle up your poison from the lengthy drinks list, anything from Bloodies to Brandy Alexanders.

Best nooks and crannies for romantics... In addition to its classic look—brick walls, terra-cotta floors, wood beams, straw baskets, strands of garlic hanging from walls—**El Mollete** is distinctive for such arty touches as trees painted on the ceiling and marvelous bullfighting caricatures on the walls. Taped cool jazz wafts through the space, the attractive, attitude-free 20-somethings are quite approachable, and the tiny balcony, with only a couple of tables, is ultra-private. At **Kairós**, untamed cocktails, unpretentious atmosphere, ocher walls with imaginative tracery, cracked marble floors, and dried floral arrangements complete the image of a picture-book romantic evening out; the mezzanine is especially enticing, as pop vocals play softly and the stylish 30-somethings murmur sweet everythings in each other's ears. The side bar of **La Rotonda**, reminiscent of an English manor library, is the perfect place to seal a deal; from the whispers and darting looks, it's no stranger to liaisons of both a business and romantic nature. The sweetly authentic **Las Cuevas del Sésamo** is a throwback to the more romantic days of *The Student King* and other operettas; if it weren't for the distinctly urban guerrilla gear, you'd half expect someone to break out with a misty-eyed serenade. It looks so impossibly perfect it could be a film set, right down to the black-and-white tile floors, checked tablecloths, cheap but potent sangria, and sing-alongs at the piano. **Alhama** is downright seductive, with recessed hand-painted arches, satin pillows, Tiffany-style lamps, and embroidered antimacassars. An alluring yet unself-conscious set listening to the latest wave of Spanish make-out music. **Gayarre** boasts the kind of suffocatingly tasteful decor a retired madam might use to win over her former clients' wives. Voluptuous describes the interior, if not the crowd.

Living by their wits... **Libertad 8** revived the dying art of *cuentacuentos* (storytelling), with regular nights set aside for revisionist folk tales or recitals of Poe's poetry. Usually several *cuentistas* take the stage; some invite the audience to suggest a topic and they then improvise the beginning, middle, and end within a set time limit. It's warm and inviting, right down to the lace curtains and fringe lamps. **Candilejas** means limelight, as in the Chaplin classic. The terminally hip audience could easily grab the limelight themselves, but prefer to enjoy the evening's entertainment. If you *habla*, you'll howl at the barbed political sketches and saucy cabaret ditties.

The debating club meets here... The *tertulias* at **Café Gijón** are among the fiercest and most formal in town. It even throws a hotly contested annual short story competition (no, not for the worst Hemingway imitation). A charming Art Nouveau bastion of the literary set, **Café Manuela** hosts regular *tertulias* in English, French, and Spanish; storytelling sessions, music recitals, and poetry reading are also on the calendar. *Tertulias* have raged at the Socialist **Café Comercial** since before the Spanish Civil War, and they continue to spread like forest fires, especially among the literary types who now frequent it. Though there's definitely a feminist bias in the readings and *tertulias* at **La Madriguera**, recent topics at their regularly scheduled debates have ranged from "The Role of

Women in Today's Society" to "The Current State of Scientific Investigation in Spain." If you don't want to join in the fray, you can order one of their delicious daily specialties, peruse the bookshelves for political or cultural tomes, or just sit and admire the abstract take on Velázquez's masterpiece *Las Meninas* that dominates the space. **Círculo de Bellas Artes** is a favorite among intelligentsia (who spout off in torrid *tertulias* as regularly as Old Faithful) and local bureaucrats alike. As the name suggests, culture vultures convene here regularly, animatedly discussing the current state of the arts—or the sperm whale—in the ornate yet unpretentious surroundings.

Where to study students... At the dirt-cheap **Las Cuevas del Sésamo**, sayings by writers and artists as diverse as Braque and Santillana, as well as clever graffiti (*Prohibido entrar a quien sepa geometría*—"*Entry forbidden to anyone who knows geometry*") are stenciled on the arches, while dusty books line the stairwell. The university crowd (certainly no one older than recent grad-school kids) smokes up a storm while dancing in place to the latest techno/house/soul mix in the spookily neo-Gothic **Kamelot**, which sports brick arches and jack-o'-lantern lamps carved into the wood columns. The more studious, less 'tudious grad students flock to **Cardenal**: doctors-, lawyers-, and magnates-to-be line up as early as 9pm. The brick walls and wood-beamed ceiling dressed up with contemporary touches like the cool cast-iron lamps at the bar (which provide practically the only illumination in the joint). The intentionally silly **El Balcón de Rosales** occasionally throws "worst karaoke" contests. Youthful revelers whinny at the uproarious (and usually drunk) singers, and whistle at the good-looking waitstaff in tight clothes that leave little to the imagination.

Most elegant... Expect to see a star-studded crowd in the airy, Laura Ashley-ish lobby lounge of the **Bar César Ritz**, a Belle Epoque stunner (check out the dazzling recessed ceiling). After dinner, the cozy, more masculine English room is a favorite with the mover-and-cocktail-shaker bunch. Philippe Starck designed the several rooms that comprise Madrid's hottest restaurant/tapas/cocktail bar, **Teatriz**. The front room features high blond-wood chairs with plump white cushions. Another section, incorporating elements of the original theater, has vaulted ceilings and a bar eerily lit from within. Still another alternates brown-and-white marble tables with luxe white or brown leather chairs that make you feel like pawns on a chessboard. There's even a dance floor with padded white walls (for the overly energetic?), which is apt since it's about the size of an asylum cell. **La Rotonda**, the resplendent, recently restored bar in the Palace Hotel, is judiciously extravagant, representing Art Nouveau at its considerable best. It's Old-World and old-school, down to the huge potted plants (and discreetly potted customers), towering floral arrangements, tapestries so faded they must be genuine, crystal chandeliers, plush armchairs, "bland"scapes, mahogany paneling, and soaring stained glass cupola. **Candilejas** is one of Madrid's most stylish bars, with splendid genuine film posters, stills, and celeb photos (Barbra!). Admire the giant mural of the old Madrid skyline while luxuriating in the scarlet couches and ottomans that snake around immaculate white marble tables. If only the gentlemen wore black tie and monocles, **El Salón del Prado** could very well be a literary/artistic salon of the last century run by a society matron. It's simply smashing: classical sculptures, bronze sconces, crystal candelabras, taupe columns, gorgeous wainscoting, and a grand piano. It offers chamber music concerts, as well as the occasional folk singer, jazz combo, even ethnic artists from around the globe. Despite the posh air, it's quite informal. **Círculo de Bellas Artes** is a stately slice of the Belle Epoque: parquet floors, stained glass windows, frescoed ceilings, a palatial chandelier, as well as a striking sculpture of two reclining nudes.

Sidewalk cafe culture... Don't expect the stately syncopations of Ravel at **Bolero**: disco music blares so loud you can't hear yourself think at this concrete beach party, (in)famous for its Miss Castellana drag queen contests (where biting, scratching, and catcalling are the norm). The audience—equal parts glittery and trashy-flashy, discriminating in an indiscriminate, indiscreet sort of way— often outperforms the drag queens. **La Riviera** appeals to *terraza* types who appreciate its kitschy decor, bright bold colors that resemble a glossy Doris Day–Rock Hudson movie. The *terraza* of **Café Gijón** attracts a beautiful if decaying crowd who seem to have been deeded their tables and prefer to watch the sidewalk parade than join in the proceedings. **El Espejo**, a smashing Art Nouveau edifice only looks authentic: the glowing tile-and-stained glass pavilion that contains an amazing mirrored, dark wood bar and beamed ceiling was built in 1978. The *terraza* is a marvelous vantage point for watching the Recoletos/Castellana crawl. The appealing **Balcón de Rosales** is one of the most popular *terrazas* with the younger crowd, who enjoy the views of the Parque del Oeste (and its transvestite hookers).

Where the matadors hang... Bar Taurino, a big Ava Gardner and Hemingway hangout in the fifties, offers suitably atavistic decor, with polished wood tables and cherry-wood bar, red leather cushions, and glowering bull heads mounted on the walls. Today it's a cultured spot for elderly society ladies—who may well have posted photos of the great torero Manolete above their beds way back when. It really heats up during the famed San Isidro Bullfighting Festival in May, when everyone risks whiplash, craning their necks to view the current legends enter in a ceremonious sweep of gold sequins, azure tights, crimson jackets, and glittery stockings in rainbow colors. A virtual shrine to the *corrida* (bullfight), **Taberna de Antonio Sánchez** was opened in 1830 by a popular matador of the same name; all its subsequent owners have been involved in the profession, either as fighters, promoters, or journalists. It's steeped in tradition, as the zinc bar, bulls'-head trophies, fetching Spanish art naif, sherry casks, caricatures of the greats, and treasure trove of yellowing photos of bullfights, matador outfits, *banderillas* (the short, barbed lances) attest. Regulars (neighborhood locals of all ages) go rabid when they're out of the classic tapa *rabo de toro* (bull's tail). **Los Gatos** retains a delightful old-time feel, thanks to matador costumes and paintings, turn-of-the-century street lamps, painted tiles, homey wooden benches and tables (invariably packed with bullfighting aficionados discussing that day's corrida), and cats represented in virtually every artistic medium (*gatos*, the nickname for locals, means "cats").

The Bar Scene: Index

Alhama. Mudejar decor, cushy seats, subdued lighting, and soft music make this ultraromantic.... *No phone. Travesía de Trujillos, 1; Sol or Santo Domingo metro stop.* **(see p. 63)**

Alkalde. Perhaps the definitive Basque tapas bar/restaurant, resembling a chic farmhouse.... *Tel 576–33–59. Jorge Juan, 10; Serrano metro stop.* **(see p. 61)**

Almendro 13. A trendy, youthful crowd enjoys the tapas at this classic old-town pub.... *Tel 365–42–52. Almendro, 13; La Latina metro stop.* **(see p. 60)**

El Anciano Rey de los Vinos. Open since 1907. Memorable food and forgettable decor.... *Tel 532–14–73. La Paz, 4; Sol metro stop.* **(see p. 60)**

La Ardosa. Regulars still flock to Madrid's first "Irish" pub, despite the fact it looks like a glorified liquor store.... *Tel 521–49–79. Colón, 13; Tribunal metro stop.* **(see p. 55)**

Asquiniña. Though bare-bones, this is the premier place to sample Galician tapas.... *Tel 366–59–44. Plaza de Puerta Cerrada, 11; La Latina metro stop.* **(see p. 61)**

Bagatelle. A spacious, attractive, just-after-dinner dance place for yuppies of all ages and stripes.... *No phone. Barquillo, 45; Chueca metro stop.* **(see p. 56)**

El Balcón de Rosales. Characterful Madrid funspot known for kitschy karaoke and comedy tryouts; the *terraza* is SRO in warm weather.... *Tel 541–74–40. Paseo del Pintor Rosales; Argüelles metro spot.* **(see p. 64)**

Bar César Ritz. Madrid's most celebrity-ridden haunt, where everyone expects to be treated like royalty (they often are).... *Tel 521–28–57. Hotel Ritz, Plaza de la Lealtad, 5; Banco de España metro stop.* **(see pp. 62, 64)**

Bar Cock. The martinis at this sleek power-broker spot are the best in town, and the clientele—even the artsy-fartsy types—believe they're better than you are.... *Tel 532–28–26. Reina, 16; Gran Vía metro stop.* **(see pp. 51, 62)**

Bar Taurino. This cozy mini-tiered space is a shrine to Manolete, the greatest matador of the 1950s.... *Tel 531–45–00. Hotel Tryp Reina Victoria, Plaza Santa Ana, 14; Sevilla or Antón Martín metro stop.* **(see p. 66)**

Berlín Cabaret. The best drag shows in town (and the people-watching ain't bad, either).... *Tel 366–20–34. Costanilla de San Pedro, 11; La Latina metro stop.* **(see p. 50)**

Black and White. Hi-tech gay bar, busy early with hilarious but hot "boylesque" shows.... *Tel 531–11–41. Libertad, 34; Chueca metro stop.* **(see p. 54)**

Bocaíto. The look is traditional, the tapas anything but at this trendy "mixed" Chueca spot.... *Tel 532–12–19. Libertad, 6; Chueca metro stop. Closed Sun and second half of Aug.* **(see p. 59)**

Bodega de Roberto el Pirata. A tin skull and crossbones welcomes you into this modish haunt of the better-heeled grunge set.... *No phone. Conde de Xiquena, 2; Banco de España/Chueca metro stop. Closed Sun.* **(see pp. 52, 57)**

Bolero. This deliciously scandalous *terraza* is a fashionable venue for record launches, fashion shows, and drag contests.... *No phone. Paseo de la Castellana, 33; Rubén Darío metro stop. Closed Oct—Apr.* **(see p. 65)**

Las Bravas. Basically a cafeteria/bar without seats. Overlook the fake wood walls, Formica, and exposed piping, and order their trademark tapas creation, *patatas bravas*.... *Tel 521–51–41. Pasaje Matheu, 5; Sol metro stop.* **(see p. 60)**

El Brillante. This tapas cafeteria is continually noisy, especially

around 6 or 7am when night-crawlers stagger in for a revivifying coffee.... *Tel 528–69–66. Glorieta del Emperador
Carlos V, 8; Atocha metro stop.* **(see p. 61)**

Café Acuarela. This paean to high kitsch attracts a diverse,
non-cruisy gay crowd.... *Tel 570–69–07. Gravina, 10;
Chueca metro stop. Closed Sun.* **(see p. 55)**

Café Comercial. Turn-of-the-century Madrid tradition popular
throughout the evening.... *Tel 521–56–55. Glorieta de
Bilbao, 7; Bilbao metro stop.* **(see pp. 53, 63)**

Café Figueroa. Relaxed gay spot is popular early evenings for a
quick drink, not for a quickie.... *Tel 521–16–73. Augusto
Figueroa, 17; Chueca metro stop. Closed Sun.* **(see p. 55)**

Café Galdós. The gay/lesbian clientele at this quiet oasis tends
to be more mature and settled (if not settled down).... *Tel
532–12–86. Benito Pérez Galdós, 1; Chueca metro stop.
Closed Sun.* **(see p. 55)**

Café Gijón. A legendary, always packed, hangout that puts on
few airs.... *Tel 521–54–25. Paseo de Recoletos, 21; Banco
de España metro stop.* **(see pp. 53, 63, 65)**

Café Manuela. Notable for holding weekly *tertulias* on a wide
range of topics in various languages, and for its grand decor
and amiable atmosphere.... *Tel 531–70–37. San Vicente
Ferrer, 29; Tribunal metro stop.* **(see p. 63)**

Café La Troje. Popular gay-male hangout before the night out offi-
cially starts. Lesbians are also made to feel at home here.... *No phone. Pelayo, 26; Chueca metro stop.* **(see p. 55)**

Calentito. Steamy Latino music bar with nutty decor is packed
late weekend nights.... *No phone. Jacometrezo, 15; Callao
or Santo Domingo metro stop.* **(see pp. 51, 58)**

Candela. Flamenco posters and photos attest to its enduring
popularity among the nomadic set, including simply the
roaming gypsies of Madrid's bar scene.... *Tel 467–33–82.
Olmo, 2; Antón Martín metro stop.* **(see p. 52)**

Candilejas. Fashionable bar with poetry readings, guitarists,

THE BAR SCENE ☽ INDEX

and scathing satires.... *Tel 365–55–45. Bailén, 16; Ópera or La Latina metro stop.* **(see pp. 63, 65)**

Capote. Punkers and yupsters alike dance to a sensational blues/reggae/samba/trance mix at this intentionally over-designed bar.... *Tel 319–01–38. Santa Teresa, 3; Alonso Martinez metro stop.* **(see p. 52)**

Cardenal. A hot music mix, pretty young things on the prowl, and cheap drinks are the recipe for success here.... *Cardenal Cisneros, 32; Bilbao metro stop.* **(see p. 64)**

Casa Labra. Historic (founded in 1860) and always packed at tapas time with locals and tourists alike.... *Tel 532–14–05. Tetùán, 12; Sol metro stop.* **(see p. 53)**

Cervecería Alemana. Imperative stop on the tapas-for-tourists trail.... *Tel 429–70–33. Plaza de Santa Ana, 6; Sevilla or Antón Martín metro stop.* **(see p. 58)**

Chicote. Truly legendary retro-chic bar that is usually the first stop in what locals jokingly call the "Bermuda Triangle" of cocktail bars (the other two being Bar Cock and Del Diego just around the corner).... *Tel 532–67–37. Gran Vía, 21; Gran Vía metro stop. Closed Sun.***(see pp. 52, 53, 58, 62)**

La Ciberteca. A relaxed place to Websurf.... *Tel 556–56–03, General Perón, 32 bajos; Lima metro stop. Computer time: 675 ptas. per half hour, 500 ptas. for guests under 21.* **(see p. 59)**

Círculo de Bellas Artes. Hallowed ground for both artistic and commercial types, with low-key ambience, low-priced tapas, haute decor.... *Tel 531–85–03; Marqués de Casa Riera, 2; Banco de España metro stop.* **(see pp. 64, 65)**

Cruising. The "feeling out and up" process continues through-out the night, with back rooms is as busy as Grand Central station at rush hour.... *Tel 521–51–43. Benito Pérez Galdós, 5; Chueca metro stop.* **(see p. 53)**

Las Cuevas del Sésamo. Romantic, student-bohemian base-ment bar.... *Tel 465–65–24. Príncipe, 7; Sevilla or Sol metro stop.* **(see pp. 63, 64)**

Del Diego. A former Chicote waiter opened this trendy sixties-style cocktail bar.... *Tel 523–31–06. Reina, 12; Gran Vía metro stop.* **(see p. 62)**

Errota-Zar. The cozy basement of this superior Basque restaurant is an unassuming jewel of a tapas bar.... *Tel 531–25–64. Jovellanos, 3 bajos; Sevilla metro stop.* **(see p. 60)**

El Espejo. A old standby for drinks or tapas after work, and later in the evening for a *cafecito*.... *Tel 308–23–47. Paseo de Recoletos, 31; Colón metro stop.* **(see pp. 61, 66)**

Fábrica de Pan. The bands and DJs are some of the savviest in town, alert to the latest indie trends.... *No phone. San Bartolomé, 21; Chueca metro stop.* **(see p. 57)**

Los Gabrieles. Unmemorable tapas, busloads of tourists, and a smug, sniggering waitstaff detract from the most exquisite and most photographed tile work in Madrid.... *Tel 429–62–61. Echegaray, 17; Sevilla metro stop.* **(see p. 57)**

Los Gatos. A local favorite for its high-quality, low-priced tapas (succulent *gambas al ajillo*—shrimp in robust garlic sauce) and amiable ambience.... *Tel 429–30–67. Jesús, 2; Antón Martín metro stop.* **(see p. 66)**

Gayarre. Spacious and soaring (by Madrid standards): airplane hangar where affluent, lonely 30-to-60-somethings take flight.... *Tel 564–25–15. Paseo de la Castellana, 118; Nuevos Ministerios metro stop.* **(see p. 63)**

La Gloria. Offers the ABCs (and D) of hipdom: Almodóvar ambience, Beautiful people, Creativity, and Decor.... *Tel 542–40–03. Vergara, 10; Ópera metro stop.* **(see p. 50)**

Houston's Cattle Company. Taped C&W music drones at this temple to American kitsch.... *Tel 542–69–64. Silva, 1; Santo Domingo metro stop.* **(see p. 62)**

The Irish Rover. The facade of this fern pub is emerald green, and there's Guinness on tap.... *Tel 555–76–71. Avda. de Brasil, 7; Lima metro stop.* **(see p. 55)**

Isis. Few bars in Madrid cater almost exclusively to lesbians.

THE BAR SCENE ☽ INDEX

This dark, sexy hole rectifies the problem (though men are welcome).... *No phone. Plaza de Chueca, 10; Chueca metro stop.* **(see p. 54)**

José Luis. The first and still first-rate Salamanca branch of this stereotypical tapas bar is a de rigueur Madrid experience.... *Tel 563–09–58. Serrano, 89; Avda. de América metro stop.* **(see pp. 56, 61)**

Kairós. An enchanting spot, with subdued music, fancy decor, dim lighting, and a smart set.... *Tel 361–04–25. Nuncio, 19; La Latina metro stop.* **(see p. 62)**

Kamelot. As at all its neighbors, lines gather from 9pm(!) on to squeeze into the immense Kamelot.... *No phone. Cardenal Cisneros, 12; Bilbao metro stop.* **(see p. 64)**

King Creole. Irrepressible teeny-boppers nod their heads to the fab (mostly fifties) mix....*Tel 522–24–52. San Vicente Ferrer, 7; Tribunal metro stop.* **(see p. 56)**

Kingston's. Trendy yet mellow Almodóvar (yes, him again) hang-out, but usually without his hangers-on.... *Tel 521–15–68. Barquillo, 29; Chueca metro stop.* **(see p. 58)**

Lerranz. Has a more refined (read haughty) air than most nearby Santa Ana establishments.... *Tel 429–12–06. Echegaray, 26; Sevilla metro stop.* **(see p. 60)**

Lhardy. Popular with the wealthy and powerful—those with discriminating palates.... *Tel 522–22–07. Carrera de San Jerónimo, 8; Sol metro stop. Closed Sun night.* **(see p. 60)**

Libertad 8. Hosts storytelling sessions, as well as comedy and cabaret evenings.... *Tel 532–11–50. Libertad, 8; Chueca or Banco de España metro stop.* **(see p. 63)**

Louie Louie. Resembles a speakeasy, replete with peephole, but the policy is open door at this shrine to classic rock-and-roll.... *No phone. La Palma, 43; Tribunal metro stop.* **(see p. 56)**

La Lupe. Cool, laid-back, indispensable part of the "alternative" gay scene. Run by the Radical Gai (Act Up and Queer

Nation rolled into one).... *Tel 527–50–19. Torrecilla del Leal, 12; Antón Martín metro stop.* **(see p. 54)**

La Madriguera. This open-door lesbian/feminist bookstore-cafe is lovely and lively.... *Tel 559–33–45. Santiago, 3; Ópera metro stop.* **(see pp. 55, 63)**

Matador. Wild and woolly hotspot rocks continuously through the evening.... *No phone. La Cruz, 39; Sol metro stop.*
(see p. 51)

Mito. Laid-back but not out-to-get-laid gay/lesbian bar.... *No phone. Plaza de Chueca, 6; Chueca metro stop.*
(see p. 53)

Moby Dick. Yupsters listen to live folk, blues, pop, and lite rock most nights, trying to harpoon a one-nighter.... *Tel 555–76–71. Avda. de Brasil, 5; Lima metro stop.* **(see p. 56)**

El Mojito. Tony bar for gays and straights, not style-conscious at all (though with the exception of Almodóvar and his cronies, those over 40 may feel obsolete).... *No phone. Olmo, 6; Antón Martín metro stop.* **(see pp. 50, 54)**

El Mollete. Atmospheric, creatively decorated respite from the tourist hordes overrunning the Plaza Mayor.... *No phone. La Bola, 2; Santo Domingo metro stop.* **(see p. 62)**

El Moskito. Another mixed, alternative gay club with a slightly heavier lesbian bias than its Lavapiés cohorts.... *No phone. Torrecilla del Leal, 13; Antón Martín metro stop.* **(see p. 54)**

Museo del Jamón. The "Museum of Ham," which refers not to porky patrons but to the specialty of the house.... *No phone. Carrera de San Jerónimo, 10; Sol metro stop.* **(see p. 61)**

Nell's. This luxurious yet snug (not to mention smug) pijo enclave would be romantic if it weren't for the nonstop pounding disco music.... *Tel 562–49–54. López de Hoyos, 25; Avda. de América metro stop. Closed Mon.* **(see p. 50)**

Net Café. Cyber-trekkies stare vacantly at computer screens and music videos here; the music is so loud you wonder how they can concentrate.... *Tel 594–09–99. San Bernardo,*

THE BAR SCENE ☾ INDEX

81; San Bernardo metro stop. Computer time: 500 ptas. per half hour. **(see p. 59)**

No Fun. Beware of perching too comfortably on the ragged stools or steel beer barrels: the place defines grunge in every way.... *Espíritu Santo, 7; Tribunal metro stop.* **(see p. 59)**

Oba-Oba. The sensational drinks and dancers will quickly make you forget you're not in Rio at this pathetic imitation of a Brazilian nightclub.... *No phone. Jacometrezo, 14; Santo Domingo metro stop.* **(see p. 58)**

Old Fox Tavern. This Irish/American enclave is a comfortable, mellow sports hangout.... *Tel 308–33–09. Hortaleza, 118; Alonso Martínez metro stop.* **(see p. 55)**

Peláez. Despite its ritzy Salamanca location, this place is utterly unpretentious, and the tapas and crafts, both from around Spain, are sublime.... *Tel 575–87–24. Lagasca, 61; Serrano metro stop. Closed Sun, Aug.* **(see p. 61)**

Rick's. This elegant gay bar is a welcome antidote to the sleaze permeating the Chueca barrio. Its idea of a back room is a cozy area with a foosball table and lavender walls.... *No phone. Clavel, 8; Gran Vía metro stop.* **(see p. 53)**

La Riviera. Top mid-sized concert venue (see The Club Scene) is also arguably the most popular *terraza* outside the Castellana, with several airy, glossily designed bars.... *Tel 365–24–15. Paseo Bajo de la Virgen del Puerto, at juncture with Puente de Segovia; Puerta del Angel metro stop.* **(see p. 65)**

La Rotonda. If you like bastions of hotel civility like New York's Plaza or London's Connaught, you'll feel right at home.... *Tel 360–80–00. Palacé Hotel, Plaza de las Cortes, 7; Banco de España metro stop.* **(see pp. 62, 65)**

El Salón del Prado. Come to savor the refined yet relaxed ambience and delicious tapas or later, an equally fine menu of live music.... *Tel 429–33–61. Prado, 4; Sevilla metro stop.* **(see p. 65)**

San Mateo Seis. A typical Malasaña joint, with cuttings from rock magazines, pool tables, loud music, and loaded "dance floor" (and customers).... *Tel 535–45–35. San Mateo, 6; Tribunal metro stop.* **(see p. 57)**

Star's Café-Dance. The mélange of alternative, serious, and frivolous fashion rags in various languages on the magazine racks reflects the trendy crowd at this disco-bar.... *Tel 522–27–12. Marqués de Valdeiglesias, 5; Banco de España or Gran Vía metro stop.* **(see p. 52)**

Taberna de Antonio Sánchez. Madrid's oldest tavern offers incomparable bullfight atmosphere.... *Tel 539–78–28. Mesón de Paredes, 13; Tirso de Molina metro stop.* **(see p. 66)**

La Tapería. Bustling university hangout presents an A-Plus combo of good music, better food, and cheap prices in traditional brick/wood/tile surroundings.... *No phone. San Bernardo, 84; San Bernardo metro stop.* **(see p. 61)**

Tatoom Road. "Boom" would be an equally appropriate name, given the blasting sound system at this airy, rich-young-thing saloon.... *Tel 556–28–33. Avda. de Brasil, 3; Lima metro stop. Closed Mon.* **(see p. 56)**

Teatriz. As the name suggests, this is an old theater, converted (by Philippe Starck) into an ostentatiously hip, post-modern space where everyone seems to be "on."... *Tel 577–53–79. Hermosilla, 15; Serrano metro stop.* **(see pp. 61, 64)**

Top XI. Good, if thunderous, music and a positively joyous happy hour help explain the otherwise inexplicable popularity of this unassuming gay dump.... *No phone. Augusto Figueroa, 16; Chueca metro stop.* **(see p. 54)**

Torero. Everyone here negotiates the crowd, the bar, and the opposite sex with equal élan.... *Tel 523–11–29. Cruz, 26; Sol metro stop. Closed Sun, Mon.* **(see p. 56)**

Torito. A minuscule temple of kitsch that draws a lively crowd, most of whom sashay in place to the flamenco and rumba.... *Tel 532–77–99. Pelayo, 4; Chueca metro stop.* **(see p. 51)**

La Trucha. Stereotypically Andalusian, with brown-and-white arches, hand-painted Sevillan plates, and strings of garlic bulbs, which clues you into the tapas specialties.... *Tel*

429–58–33. Manuel Fernández y González, 3; Sol metro stop. **(see p. 60)**

Truco. As with most Madrid lesbian bars, this one also gets a sizable contingent of gay men, though gender and even sexual orientation don't matter once the music starts.... *Tel 532–89–21. Plaza Chueca, 4; Chueca metro stop.* **(see p. 54)**

Tupperware. Neo-hippie, ultra-cool bar whose regulars are anything but plastic and suburban.... *No phone. Corredera Alta de San Pablo; Tribunal metro stop.* **(see p. 59)**

Vaivén. An intimate balcony rings the floor, and there are discreetly spotlit areas so the yuppie crowd can see who they're kissing.... *Tel 319–28–18. Travesía San Mateo, 1; Tribunal metro stop.* **(see p. 56)**

La Venancia. This sherry and tapas bar is always charming and lively, despite the gruff waiters who've clearly seen it all.... *Tel 429–73–13. Echegaray, 7; Sevilla metro stop.* **(see p. 60)**

La Vía Láctea. The grunge pioneer of Madrid's live music bars.... *Tel 446–75–81. Velarde, 18; Tribunal metro stop.*
(see p. 57)

Villa Rosa. Intricate Arabesque arches and tile work adorn this hopping, happening club.... *Tel 521–36–89. Plaza de Santa Ana, 15; Sol or Sevilla metro stop. Closed Sun.* **(see p. 58)**

Viva Madrid. You'll come here for the tile work, though the tapas are actually appetizing and reasonably priced.... *Tel 429–36–40. Manuel Fernández y González; Sol metro stop.* **(see p. 57)**

Why Not? The crowd is as mixed as it gets (especially weekends), the gossip is primo, and seventies and eighties icons like Abba and George Michael chirp cheerfully in the background.... *Tel 523—05–81. San Bartolomé, 6; Gran Vía metro stop.* **(see p. 51)**

Zúkero. A sterile, stand-and-pose yuppie-teria where you'll be deafened by the standard EuroPop wailing from the speakers.... *Tel 448–56–46. San Bernardo, 90; San Bernardo metro stop.* **(see p. 56)**

3

the arts

Far more than roses in teeth
and clicking
castanets, Madrid's cultural
scene offers a wide
spectrum of dance, music,
and theater. Operaphiles
sing the praises of the

country that produced Plácido Domingo, José Carreras, and Montserrat Caballé, all of whom perform here regularly. Any given week, those who habla español can choose from Spanish playwrights like Calderón de la Barca, Lope de Vega, and García Lorca; revivals of classics by Shakespeare, Strindberg, and Beckett; contemporary British dramatists like David Hare and Dennis Potter; the great Italian Socialist monologist Dario Fo; or new American absurdists like Nicky Silver. The theaters themselves range from experimental black boxes seating fewer than 100 to extravagant Art Nouveau edifices.

The visual arts scene is even more vibrant. Spain scored a coup when it finally wrested Picasso's *Guernica* from New York's MOMA; it now rests comfortably in the **Museo Nacional Centro de Arte Reina Sofía**, which was constructed in 1990 to celebrate Madrid's anointing as Europe's Cultural Capital of 1992. While the great Prado and Thyssen-Bornemisza museums close by 7pm, the Reina Sofía remains open late, as do the many collections that various corporations and individual benefactors have contributed to Madrid's cultural coffers. The **Parque de Retiro** (see Hanging Out) chimes in with three neo-classical exhibition spaces. The gallery scene has been taken over by a group of enterprising women with vision, taste, and daring. Proving that Madrid retains its chauvinist element, they're nicknamed *la mafia de las bragas* (*bragas* are bloomers, as in 19th-century ladies' undergarments; the term is derived from *bragaza*, which means hen-pecked, so draw your own conclusions).

Despite grumbles from the arts establishment about decreased government subsidies, Madrid's record for cultural promotion is enviable. Several major festivals are held annually (see Hanging Out), including **Veranos de la Villa**, the **Festival de Otoño**, the experimental **Festimad**, the international art exposition **ARCO** (see Festivals in Down and Dirty) and specialized events celebrating Mozart, flamenco, jazz, and crafts.

Tickets and Information

Most box offices are open from roughly 11am to 2pm and again from 5 to 8, but the hours vary slightly from theater to theater and from season to season. Prices generally range between 1,000–5,000 ptas. for most cultural events, but they can climb to about 13,500 for opera. **FNAC** (tel 595–61–00 main branch; Preciados, 28; Callao metro stop; open

Mon–Sat 10am–10pm, Sun noon–8pm) sells tickets to theater, dance, opera, exhibitions, and concerts without commission. **Tel-Entradas** (tel 538–33–33 main branch; Paseo de Recoletos, 15; Banco de España metro stop; Mon–Sat 8am–1am, Sun 9am–1am) is a no-commission ticket agency run by the Caja de Cataluña bank; you can charge tickets via phone, or at the bank itself during normal business hours, then pick them up at the box office a half hour before the curtain. For hard-to-get tickets your only recourse, other than scalpers, is **TEYCI** (tel 576–45–32; Goya, 5–7; Serrano metro stop; open Mon–Thur 10am–2pm, 4–8pm, Fri–Sun 10am–8pm), which adds a straight 20-percent surcharge.

The weekly entertainment bible *Guía del Ocio* and the newspapers *El País, El Mundo,* and *ABC* offer complete listings of films, plays, concerts, opera, art exhibits, and dance. The free *Guiarte* is an excellent source of information on gallery exhibits; it also runs stimulating reviews, commentary, and interviews.

Timing

Unless otherwise noted, theaters are dark on Monday, and the curtain usually goes up at 7:30 or 8pm. All the galleries and museums listed here remain open until 8:30 or 9pm, and are usually closed on Sunday (though sometimes just for the evening) and Monday (except the Reina Sofía, which is closed on Tuesday). Admission is free unless otherwise indicated.

THE ARTS ⟨ INTRODUCTION

Where it's at... The most impressive, star-laden opera productions were traditionally held in the **Teatro Real** (tel 516–06–00), an exquisite neoclassical opera house on the Plaza de Oriente. City officials were foolish (or corrupt) enough to build it over an underground stream in the 1850s; it closed for renovation in 1987. Its reopening date has been pushed back every year since 1992; the current promise is for spring 1998, but don't hold your breath—they've already lost Pavarotti for *Parsifal*. The **Teatro de la Zarzuela**, a magnificent 1856 monument emulating Milan's great La Scala, has assumed the Real's place in the interim, hosting the Orquesta Sinfónica de Madrid and ballet and lieder recitals. The major classical music venue is the **Auditorio Nacional de Música**. Built in 1988, it holds both a 2,280-seat main stage and a more intimate chamber hall with 707 seats. It's home to the Orquesta y Coro (Choir) Nacional de España, and regularly welcomes leading guest conductors (Pinchas Zukerman, Zubin Mehta) and orchestras (Los Angeles Philharmonic, London Philharmonic, Amsterdam's Royal Concertgebouw). The hideously functional exterior resembles a constructivist Greco-Roman temple in unflattering dun and gray, but the acoustics, sight lines, and sound and lighting systems are superb. **Teatro Monumental** is an undistinguished mid-sized venue whose main tenant is the Orquesta y Coro de RTVE. **Centro Cultural de la Villa** is an all-in-one municipal auditorium that presents expert but unexciting modern dance, flamenco, plays, children's theater, pop concerts, contemporary Spanish art exhibits, and touring ballet companies on its two stages. The venue is remarkably comfortable, though, and the setting—just under the fountains of the Plaza Colón—magnificent. **Teatro de**

Albéniz stages select ballets, modern dance recitals, and plays; it is also the primary venue for the Festival de Otoño. **Teatro de Madrid** is a gleaming contemporary establishment that hosts leading dance companies from Spain and around the globe. Madrid's oldest theater, **Teatro Español** is an exquisitely simple structure dating from 1745; this is the place to come to for first-rate productions of modern classics. Two houses have devoted themselves to the classical Spanish repertoire: the **Teatro de la Comedia**, home of the Compañía Nacional de Teatro Clásico, and **Teatro María Guerrero**, which hosts the Centro Dramático Nacional. The **Centro Cultural Conde Duque** was originally constructed as a Palace Guard barracks in the 18th century. Its thick granite walls form three imposing art galleries, which are abutted by spacious patios used for sculpture exhibitions and a variety of classical and jazz acts.

Figaro in his own land... Opera classics with international artists and guest conductors are mounted at the **Teatro de la Zarzuela**. The homegrown zarzuela is a comic operetta that typically celebrates the deeds of those crafty, cunning, resourceful *castizos* (true madrileños). The infectious, cheerful cadences remind many of the music of Johann Strauss, Victor Herbert, W. S. Gilbert, or, at their finest, the master of bel canto, Donizetti. When the **Teatro Real** finally reopens, it will stage productions of most of the zarzuelas, as well as major opera. Perhaps the most charming way to experience zarzuela in the meantime is to go to the semi-open-air, summer-only **La Corrala**, a restored 1882 tenement creatively used as a backdrop to the lively street scenes that comprise much of the genre.

In a classical mood... Spain's supposed showpiece organization, the Orquesta y Coro Nacional de España, has been continually wracked by internal dissension, musicians' strikes, and government cutbacks in funding, lending new meaning to the term "soap opera". The fact that this major national orchestra has relied entirely on guest conductors since 1994, is scandalous. Most madrileños now feel that its main rival, the Orquesta Sinfónica de Madrid, produces work of higher caliber. The capital's third notable orchestra is the Orquesta y Coro de RTVE (the acronym for Radio and Television España). Created to perform music for broadcasting, its live concerts have ironically become Madrid's most popular (and inexpensive), and the company has gained an international reputation for its recordings of Spanish classics and zarzuelas. The finest chamber music/solo-recital venues are the smaller space of the **Auditorio Nacional de Música**, which books top performers from around the world, **La Fídula** (see The Club Scene), **Salón del Prado** (see The Bar Scene), and **Círculo de Bellas Artes** (see The Bar Scene and below). The latter is also home of the highly regarded 12-piece ensemble, Grupo Círculo, that performs new works by premier Spanish composers like Luís de Pablo and Cristóbal Halffter.

Viva Las Vegas!... Madrid has two flashy, trashy, splashy floor shows that drag in the tourists and the suburban set. **La Scala** is Spain's answer to extravagant revues like the Lido and Folies Bergères: plenty of flesh (totally topless) playing peekaboo between feathers and sequins. In addition, there are dance numbers (including adequately performed classical and folkloric ballet), fervent renditions of Spanish pop (primarily the weepy, corny, breast-beating variety), even a dash of magic and a soupçon of comedy. The room is huge and fancy, with a mirrored entrance, sweeping staircase, and art nouveau flourishes. Before and after the revue, you can enjoy pop standards courtesy of a tuxedoed piano player in the front room. **Florida Park** is lower-rent and tackier. Spanish ballet (a fusion of various dance styles predominantly set to classical Spanish music) can be enchanting, but the Florida Park version, not to mention its flamenco acts, are so exaggerated they seem melodramatic. The hokey atmosphere is enhanced by "tropical" decor—rattan, palm trees, and bright jungle fabrics. Couples in their 50s wearing a Fort Knox of gold jewelry touch-dance to a live orchestra between and after the shows. Far more refined is **Noches de Cuplé**. Olga Ramos, who is well into her eighties yet still spry and coyly flirtatious, and her daughter Olga María are the foremost exponents of the turn-of-the-century castizo songs and dances of love and courtship: *cuplés, chotis,* and *pasacalles.* Ramos is credited with keeping the *cuplé* folk tradition alive; her show has been a sentimental Madrid favorite for decades. The evening is a joyous whirl of skirts, fluttering fans, and utterly graceful gestures.

The *theatah*... The class act is the Compañía Nacional de Teatro Clásico, based in the elegant **Teatro de la Comedia**. Dedicated to keeping Spanish classics alive for modern audiences, it's certainly the peer of France's acclaimed Comedie Française. The intimate **Teatro Español** (763 seats) is the other major venue, producing excellent revivals of international classics, as well as early 20th-century Spanish dramas like *Blood Wedding*. The future of the once preeminent Centro Dramático Nacional has been threatened by budget cuts, but its home theater, the lovely neoclassical 1885 **Teatro María Guerrero**, has been restored to its original splendor. The **Teatro de la Abadía** is a spanking new facility (1995), whose two spaces present classic revivals, poetry recitals, dance, even chamber music. Many high-profile contemporary foreign works (Edward Albee's *Three Tall Women*, Dennis Potter's *Those Blue Hills*) premiere at the magnificent 19th-century **Teatro Lara**. You'll probably see Spain's future stars here: it features a training program that has become Madrid's answer to the Actors Studio. Madrid doesn't have an equivalent of the West End or Broadway, and only one theater, **Teatro Nuevo Apolo**, stages new musicals. They tend to be of the extravagantly sentimental variety, like *Les Miz* (which toured here) or anything by Andrew Lloyd-Webber. The staging aims to be equally spectacular, and perhaps by Spanish standards, succeeds. The subjects are often ambitious; recent hits included a musical depicting the life of Goya's Naked Maja (the Prado meets the Great White Way!) and the renowned Havana revue, "Tropicana." For old-style musical-comedy revues bordering on vaudeville and Spanish sex farces, check out **Teatro La Latina**.

Alternative stages... Madrid's fringe theater scene is flourishing. The actual avant-garde troupes are often ephemeral, but various venues have become known as standard-bearers. One stalwart is the experimental **Ensayo 100**, which occasionally stages English-language works and has been known to stimulate *tertulias* (salons) on subjects like the relationship of science or sports to the arts. **Sala Triángulo** is the premier venue for up-and-coming playwrights; it hosts a highly regarded Alternative Theater Festival every January, as well as children's shows and cabarets.

THE ARTS ⟨ THE LOWDOWN

Tights and tutus... Madrid's two major dance companies produce extremely short seasons in town, due to their demanding touring schedules. Ballet Nacional de España performs everything from *Swan Lake* to Spanish ballet. Like any wide-ranging menu, the work is uneven—always competent, sometimes inspired. Compañía Nacional de Danza is far more experimental, its work showing such disparate influences as José Limón, Mark Morris, and Jiri Kylian. Compañía de Victor Ullate has jetéed its way into prominence as the city's foremost neoclassical troupe, though most of the staples of the repertoire, like *Giselle,* are brought to Madrid by touring foreign companies like the Royal Ballet, the Kirov, and the New York City Ballet. Among the numerous worthy dancers and chore-ographers working in the modern vein is the Compañía de Carmen Senza, whose acrobatic choreography some-times recalls Pilobolus and Pina Bausch. The main dance venues are **Teatro de la Zarzuela**, **Teatro de Madrid**, **Centro Cultural de la Villa**, and **Teatro de Albéniz**.

Flocking to flicks... Madrid has two theaters that spe-cialize in "VO" films (that's *versión original,* meaning subtitles). **Multicines Ideal** is a drab, cramped multiplex that seems straight from a Midwestern mall, complete with well-worn seats and sticky floors, but it usually car-ries five or six commercial English-language hits. **Alphaville Cinema** is the "artier" one (as the name and coffee bar attest). Though equally dilapidated, it's more stylish, with polished wood, Deco-ish decor, and plush if tatty banquettes. They often hold lectures and discussion groups on the art of the cinema. Check the papers for larger venues screening VO films. Or simply stroll the Gran Vía, a once-grand promenade now given over to McDonald's and dance halls. Several 1920s and 1930s movie palaces remain; in addition to their entertainingly ornate facades and interiors (gilt balustrades, bas-relief carvings, Bohemian crystal chandeliers), they practice the quaint tradition of hand-painting their movie posters, many of which are true works of art.

Museum hopping... The **Museo Nacional Centro de Arte Reina Sofía** is Madrid's answer to Paris's Beaubourg: an enormous, architecturally controversial museum devot-ed to modern art (at least up to the 1980s), touring international shows, lectures, and concerts. Two steel-and-glass elevators were uneasily grafted onto the severe pinkish-gray facade of the 1781 San Carlos Hospital. Befitting a former hospital, the interior is rather sterile. Many creations are reverently allotted far too much space, and your steps echo eerily on the cold granite floors, but the structurally clean lines and soft lighting display the artwork to optimum advantage. Most people cluster around Picasso's masterpiece *Guernica*, but the museum's holdings include the most comprehensive collection of contemporary Spanish art, as well as an enviable assortment of foreign work. The roster is impressive, with major works by Juan Gris, Dalí, Miró, Picasso (the latter two are also represented by many of their finest sculptures). The museum tries to make a case for other modern Spanish "greats." But these junior artists (with the exception of Antonio Saura) suffer by comparison when stacked up against other established names. The interior courtyard has been transformed into a delightful sculpture garden. The gift shop is the best of any Madrid museums. The **Museo Arqueológico Nacional** was built in 1867 to house artifacts of the numerous cultures that overran the Iberian peninsula, from Romans to Goths to Moors. It boasts astonishing 4,000-year-old neolithic bowls in pristine condition, grislier paleolithic bones (from man to mammoth) excavated from burial sites all over Spain, and many raw, disconcertingly powerful figurines (note the Dama de Elche, presumably a fertility totem, whose gender is debatable). Avoid the glass-encased replicas of the famous cave paintings of Altamira, which attract curiosity seekers and yawning schoolkids. For a look at humankind's technological advances, stop by the **Museo del Libro**. Rather than displaying dusty, yellowing volumes of *Don Quixote* or *Life is a Dream,* this ingenious installation literally (re)vivifies books through interactive programs, holographic videos, and multimedia presentations (in Spanish, but so breathtaking they're worth a look), all contrasted with such arts as cuneiform, calligraphy, and printing. There are also related graphic, newspaper, and cartoon exhibitions. The **Círculo de Bellas Artes** is not only a gathering place for intellectuals, an atmospheric cafe, and a venue for the best contemporary musical ensembles, but a promoter of the latest trends in Spanish art. The largesse of the national phone monopoly,

Telefónica, has created **Fundación Arte y Tecnología**, which has a permanent collection of Spanish art, including masterworks by Picasso, Miró, and Tàpies. A second gallery is devoted to large-scale multimedia installations by the likes of Nam Jun Paik, while another space is devoted to changing exhibitions by names such as Tadeusz Kantor. Of the many banks supporting the arts, **Fundación La Caixa** is by far the most impressive: The spare, well-lit space is ideal for exhibiting modern Spanish works; a funkily eclectic foreign section includes holdings by visionaries as diverse as William Blake and Keith Haring. The **Centro Cultural Conde Duque** mounts high-profile theme exhibits and retrospectives, from Scandinavian contemporary art to Max Klinger prints. **Fundación Juan March** was created in 1955 by the eponymous, fabulously wealthy arts patron. In addition to co-sponsoring important international touring exhibitions, it mounts comprehensive retrospectives of modern masters like Kandinsky and Matisse or schools like De Stijl; its own private collection of contemporary Spanish art rivals that of the Reina Sofía.

The Arts: Index

Alphaville Cinema. A shrine to indie cinema, with everything scrupulously VO (subtitled) and a bohemian ambience.... *Tel 559-38-36. Martín de los Heros, 14; Ventura Rodriguez metro stop.* **(see p. 84)**

Auditorio Nacional de Música. Rather homely but technologically advanced venue; Spain's paramount but troubled Orquesta y Coro Nacional is in residence.... *Tel 337-01-00. Príncipe de Vergara, 146; Cruz del Rayo metro stop. Main season Oct–June. Closed Sun, Aug.* **(see p. 80)**

Centro Cultural Conde Duque. Large-scale exhibition and concert space.... *Tel 588-58-34. Conde Duque, 11; Ventura Rodríguez metro stop. Open Mon–Sat until 9pm, Sun until 2pm.* **(see pp. 81, 86)**

Centro Cultural de la Villa. Magnificent setting with two theaters.... *Tel 575-60-80. Plaza Colón; Colón metro stop. Open daily.* **(see pp. 80, 84)**

Círculo de Bellas Artes. Belle epoque stunner. A watering hole for artists themselves, it champions virtually all artistic media.... *Tel 531-77-00. Marqués de Casa Riera, 2; Banco de España metro stop. Open daily.* **(see pp. 82, 85)**

La Corrala. Restored 19th-century tenement building transformed into a stage for authentic zarzuela settings.... *Tribulete, 12 and Sombrerete, 13; Lavapiés metro stop. Season late July–Aug.* **(see p. 81)**

Ensayo 100. Vanguard space with daring programming, including English-language theater.... *Tel 447-94-86. Raimundo Lulio, 20; Iglesia metro stop. Closed Mon–Wed.* **(see p. 83)**

Florida Park. Somewhat campy spectaculars revolving around flamenco and ballet español; live orchestra and dancing after show.... *Tel 573–78–05. Avda. Menéndez Pelayo, at Ibiza; Ibiza metro stop. Open Mon–Sat 9pm-3am. Shows at 9pm and midnight. Dinner and show, 8.800 ptas., drink and show, 4,000 ptas. (9pm) or 2,000 ptas. (midnight).* **(see p. 82)**

Fundación Arte y Tecnología. Vast, intelligently laid-out and curated space that proves corporations can pick up the slack in arts funding.... *Tel 531–29–70. Fuencarral, 1; Gran Vía metro stop. Open until 8pm Tue–Fri.* **(see p. 86)**

Fundación la Caixa. Spain's richest bank opened its vault to create this well-considered, wide-ranging art collection.... *Tel 435–48–33. Serrano, 60; Serrano metro stop. Open until 8pm Mon, Wed–Sat.* **(see p. 86)**

Fundación Juan March. Major player on the cultural scene, with large-scale exhibitions and intimate musical evenings.... *Tel 435–42–40. Castelló, 77; Nuñez de Balboa metro stop. Closed July, Aug.* **(see p. 86)**

Multicines Ideal. Typical cramped urban multiplex (eight screens), with lousy snacks and worn seats, but first-run VO movies.... *Tel 369–25–18. Doctor Cortezo, 6; Tirso de Molina metro stop.* **(see p. 84)**

Museo Arqueológico Nacional. Comprehensively covers Spain's rich archeological legacy; usually blissfully deserted, save for the inevitable school groups.... *Tel 577–79–12. Serrano, 13; Colón metro stop.* **(see p. 85)**

Museo Nacional Centro de Arte Reina Sofía. A soulless design, but an important museum. Seminal works of Miró, Dalí, Juan Gris, and Picasso.... *Tel 467–50–62. Santa Isabel, 52; Atocha metro stop.* **(see pp. 78, 84)**

Museo del Libro. Fabulous interactive museum devoted to the love of books.... *Tel 580–78–00. Biblioteca Nacional, Paseo de Recoletos, 20; Colón metro stop.* **(see p. 85)**

Noches de Cuplé. The charming revue here is the closest thing to a turn-of-the-century Madrid music hall show.... *Tel 532–71–15. De la Palma, 51; Noviciado metro stop. Shows weekdays 11:15pm, weekends 11:45. Dinner and show 6,500 ptas., drink and show 3,000 ptas. Closed Wed, Sun.* **(see p. 82)**

Sala Triángulo. Top-notch experimental theater; occasionally mounts English-language plays.... *Tel 530–68–91. Zurita, 20; Lavapiés metro stop.* **(see p. 83)**

La Scala. Vegas meets Madrid in this glittery, Moulin Rouge–style revue.... *Tel 571–44–11. Hotel Melía Castilla, Capitán Haya, 43; Cuzco metro stop. Nightly at 10pm, Sat extra show at 12:30am. Dinner and show, 9,900 ptas; drink and show, 5,100 ptas.* **(see pp. 80, 82)**

Teatro de la Abadía. Madrid's up-and-coming theater programs a diverse season of plays, dance, chamber concerts, soloists, and poetry readings.... *Tel 448–16–27. Fernández de los Rios, 42; Quevedo metro stop.* **(see p. 83)**

Teatro de Albéniz. Much of the Festival de Otoño premiers here; also respected for its mountings of plays—classic and new—as well as dance recitals.... *Tel 531–83–11. De la Paz, 11; Sol metro stop.* **(see pp. 80, 81, 84)**

Teatro de la Comedia. Home of the superlative Compañía Nacional de Teatro Clásico.... *Tel 521–49–31. Príncipe, 14; Sol metro stop. Closed Wed and July, Aug.* **(see pp. 81, 83)**

Teatro Español. Madrid's prettiest theater, devoted to superior productions of both national and international classics.... *Tel 429–62–97. Príncipe, 25; Sol metro stop.* **(see pp. 81, 83)**

Teatro Lara. Sumptuous theater offering a wide range of classic and contemporary fare.... *Tel 521–05–52. Corredera Baja de San Pablo, 15; Callao metro stop.* **(see p. 83)**

Teatro La Latina. Specializes in old-fashioned comedies and revues.... *Tel 365–28–35. Plaza de la Cebada, 2; La Latina metro stop. Closed Mon, Tue.* **(see p. 83)**

Teatro de Madrid. Lavish contemporary theater with a vast stage and ideal acoustics and sight lines. Excellent dance and drama.... *Tel 730–49–22. Avda. de la Illustración; Barrio del Pilar metro stop.* **(see pp. 81, 84)**

Teatro María Guerrero. Headquarters of the esteemed Centro Dramático Nacional.... *Tel 319–47–69. Tamayo y Baus, 4; Colón metro stop. Shows daily.* **(see pp. 81, 83)**

Teatro Monumental. The space is neither beautiful nor technologically advanced, but the Orquesta y Coro RTVE is staking a claim to become the city's leading symphony orchestra.... *Tel 429–81–19. Atocha, 65; Antón Martín metro stop. Main season Oct–May.* **(see p. 80)**

Teatro Nuevo Apolo. The only place to see Spanish musicals (don't expect *Rent*).... *Tel 429–36–95. Plaza Tirso de Molina, 1; Tirso de Molina metro stop. Closed Sun, Mon, and Aug.*
(see p. 83)

Teatro Real. Scheduled to reopen in spring 1998, *the* opera house of Madrid hosts major productions.... *Tel 516–06–00. Plaza de Oriente, Ópera metro stop.*
(see pp. 80, 81)

Teatro de la Zarzuela. Beautiful historic theater, home to serious opera, the Orquesta Sinfónica, ballet and zarzuela performances.... *Tel 429–82–25. Jovellanos, 4; Sevilla metro stop. Main season Jan–July.* **(see pp. 80, 81, 84)**

hanging out

"Hanging out" virtually
defines the madrileño temperament. *Every* spot in
Madrid seems to have been
designed as a place to
lounge, relax, socialize—
especially the bars,

restaurants, and clubs. Certain plazas are focal points for activity (or lack thereof). The Puerta del Sol, the exact geographic center of Spain, is the equivalent of Picadilly Circus or Times Square, a hub for traffic and loitering, its lovely neoclassical buildings sadly discolored by soot despite a recent renovation. Plaza Santa Ana and Plaza Mayor are the big tourist magnets, lined with bars and cafes. Students and skinheads congregate in Plaza dos de Mayo, Glorieta de Bilbao, Plaza de Santa Barbara, and Plaza de los Cubos.

But beyond the bustle, noise, and traffic still exists a living breathing city, with real people going about their business. A moment will come in your ramblings when they cease being merely a snapshot. We can't tell you where—there isn't an address—it's a state of mind you must discover for yourself. A small playground at twilight is filled with scabby-kneed kids playing *fútbol,* women in curlers shyly flirting with butchers still in their bloody aprons, and old Francoists quarreling over dominoes. A *muchacho* strums his guitar in a tranquil tree-choked plaza, kneeling before a woman with cascading raven hair, her hourglass figure a relic of some hip-happier time. She listens attentively in the still, sultry air, fanning herself lightly and every so often taking a cube of ice from her cup, dripping it down the front of her blouse, then running her cool wet hand across his forehead. It sounds like an absurdly magical parody of Figaro and his serenade. Yet it can still happen.

Where to Promenade... Madrid sports a rather somber architectural style wildly at odds with its freewheeling ambience. But the compact *Ciudad Vieja* (Old Quarter), a two-mile stretch bordered by the Prado Museum on the east and the Royal Palace on the west, is a delight to wander, especially the cobblestoned, arcaded Plaza Mayor, one of Europe's most stately squares. Constructed in 1619, this is the centerpiece of what historians call Madrid of the Asturias (Austrias) or the Hapsburgs, referring to the dynasty that ruled Spain (and much of Europe and the New World) in the 16th and 17th centuries. The Plaza's famous entry is the Arco de Cuchilleros, which also accesses a typically narrow twisting street of the same name lined with *mesones,* restaurants whose names indicate their specialty, from mushrooms to tortillas. A five-minute walk to the east, the **Plaza Santa Ana** serves as Madrid's Trafalgar Square, right down to the pigeons blanketing the fountain and trees; the beautiful 1583 facade of the Teatro Español faces down the glass exterior of the Reina Victoria Hotel (a legendary Hemingway hangout—he set the final scene of *The Sun Also Rises* here).

West of the Plaza Mayor (along the Calle Mayor) you'll pass the charming **Plaza de la Villa** on the left. This space is dominated by two ravishing edifices: the 1629 brick City Hall, topped with spindly spires on its corners, and the 1537 Casa de Cisneros, its facade embellished with ornate sculptures. Head west to **Calle Bailén**. To the left is a viaduct that overlooks a yawning urban chasm, and tiny **Las Vistillas park**, whose cafes offer the best sunset views in Madrid, thanks to its elevation. Double back north on Bailén to the area known as **Madrid of the Bourbons**, After the great dynasty that presided over Spain in the 17th and 18th centuries. The architecture here sports distinctive Baroque flourishes, epitomized by the florid balustrades and Corinthian columns of the 1764 Royal Palace. Across the street is the delightful garden-filled Plaza de Oriente, and its Teatro Real, the opera house (see The Arts). The adjoining boulevards of the **Paseo del Prado**, **Paseo de Recoletos**, and the southern part of the **Paseo de la Castellana**, all split by a lovely greenbelt, are Madrid's closest approximation to Fifth Avenue or the Champs Elysées: an unbroken architectural and horticultural chain of conspicuous consumption. The southern end of Paseo del Prado is marked by the imposing iron-glass-and-steel **Atocha Railway Station** (which imaginatively incorporates a 2,000-square-foot indoor tropical garden). Just to the east are the **Jardín Botánico** (Botanical Gardens; tel 420–30–17; Plaza de Murillo; Atocha metro stop; open 10am–9pm), created in 1781 for King Charles III, with magnificent rose arbors and more than 30,000 plants, many from the New World, all formally arranged. One block further east Calle de Alfonso XII fronts the enchanting **Parque del Retiro** (open until 10pm), which is adorned with impressive fountains (the Fallen Angel, the Turtles, and the glorious Artichoke), sculptures from neoclassical equestrian to Art Nouveau, and three stunning exhibition halls: the 1887 Crystal Palace, which is reflected in the boating lake (scheduled to reopen in mid-1998); the enterprising art space Casa de Vacas (tel 373–34–81; open until 9pm); and the neo-Renaissance brick-and-tile glass-roofed Palacio de Velázquez (known for touring art exhibits). Walking North one will find the **Plaza Cánovas del Castillo** and its breathtaking 1780 Neptune Fountain, flanked by the Cortes (parliament), Palace Hotel, and the phenomenal neoclassical palace of the Duque de Villahermosa. The southern end of Madrid's superlative Prado Museum begins here, continuing north to the **Plaza de la Lealtad**, defined by the elegant 1908 Hotel Ritz, the 1777 Apollo Fountain (depicting the four romping seasons), the Dos de Mayo Obelisk commemorating the 1808 peasant revolt against Bonaparte, and the stately Bolsa (Stock Exchange). The Paseo de Prado concludes at the eye-popping **Plaza de la Cibeles**, whose centerpiece fountain depicts the Greek goddess of fertility astride a chariot drawn by two lions; the plaza is dominated by the wedding-cake tiers of the Palacio de Comunicaciones (see Down and Dirty, Mail). Paseo de Recoletos, which leads from the Plaza, is noted for its famed cafes El Espejo and Gijón (see The Bar Scene). The avenue culminates in the unusual **Plaza de Colón**, a controversial 1970s development that includes a jazzy basement cafe, a vast performing arts space (see The Arts), and huge slabs of graffiti-laden concrete masquerading as abstract monuments to Columbus. From here, the **Paseo de la Castellana** leads through terraza-l and to commercial Madrid and the surpassingly ugly soaring skyscrapers of the **Azca** complex, of which madrileños are inordinately proud. This unfortunate patch of modern urban development includes the stark white 43-story Torre Picasso, the bronzed glass headquarters of Banco Bilbao-Vizcaya, and the circular 30-story Torre Europa.

Walk on the wild side... If it's higher-class "massage parlors" you're after you'll have to head to the commercial northern section of Madrid. The biggest concentration is on **Orense**, **Capitán Haya**, and (in ironic, dubious tribute) the street named for the discoverer of penicillin, **Calle Dr. Fleming**. Remember that penicillin may not help if you practice unsafe sex with the hookers. The pricier prostitutes hang out near the Eurobuilding. **Calle Montera**, **Puerta del Sol**, **Desengaño**, **Ballesta** (a drug-dealing street), and the no longer grand **Gran Vía** resemble pre-Disney Times Square late at night. Male hustlers, most of whom look young and malnourished enough to star in a CK One ad, ply their trade (some of it classically rough—beware) on **Almirante**. Madrid's conservative government hopes to limit all prostitution to the Casa de Campo where one of Madrid's most amusing street scenes is played out by the Teleférico (cable car) when the transvestite and transsexual hookers congregate. The action begins at around 4am, when the "girls" remove their stilettos and cool their heels in the adjacent Puerta San Vicente fountain, gossiping with sharp tongues and keeping an even sharper lookout for johns and police. You can also one-stop shop in the newspapers; all three (*ABC, El País,* and *El Mundo*) hold seemingly endless advertisements for escorts (for the non-Spanish speaker: *jovencito/a* is delectably young–but of age, *guapo/a* means hot, sexy, and *superdotadísimo/a* is, uh, well endowed, and, obviously, refers to either sex).

Going going go-go... Madrid has more topless bars than you can shake a…stick at. The heavy hitters hit on dancers (they're too refined to be called strippers) at **Nuit Madrid** (tel 555–31–31; Orense, 10; Nuevos Ministerios metro stop; open from 7pm). Black walls, mirrors, silver lamé cushions, Doric columns, and Roman busts give this strip joint an air of opulent decadence. It hosts lots of theme "fiesta" nights: masquerades (best costume prizes for audience), horror, rodeo, carnival, wet T-shirts, "fashion shows" for the S&M set or lace lingerie, and bodybuilder competitions, lest the gals feel left out. It's a preferred venue for bachelor/ette parties, celebrity pimping, and even record launches. Professional describes both the crowd and ladies at **Mundo Fantástico** (tel 528–77–27; Atocha, 80; Antón Martín metro stop; open 10pm–4am). This all-in-one sex supermarket offers strippers clinging to gangways, peep show booths (you can choose from the menu of feminine pulchritude for private showings), video rooms, live sex shows (including ménages à trois, JO, S&M, and lesbian acts), and a sex shop selling condoms (in assorted sizes, colors, and flavors), videos, magazines, vibrators, dildos, handcuffs, and provocative lingerie. On the seedier side is the dinky, dingy **Club Topless Mundial** (Agustín Figueroa, 40; Chueca metro stop; open from 6pm), a place so lilliputian you can't help but receive a lap dance. The flashing sign alone—a mermaid sipping a fruit punch—is a hoot, a testament to fifties neon artistry. The surly *señoritas*, shrouded in shawls to keep them warm between sets, sit with arms defiantly crossed and legs defiantly open. **Kabaret** (tel 405–17–21; Sambara, 55; Quintana metro stop; open from 7pm) is the most reputable "for ladies only" erotic bar. It rarely gets as wild as Chippendale's; in fact, management swears nuns have been sighted.

Browsing for books... **Casa del Libro** (tel 521–21–13; Gran Vía, 29; Gran Vía metro stop; open Mon–Sat until 8:30pm) is *the* Madrid bookstore, with five levels, its own imprint, and a vast selection of books in a dozen languages. A Barnes and Noble superstore (without the latte), it's also a hangout for foreign students, and salespeople won't disturb you if you settle down to read in one of the cushy armchairs in the various nooks.

Evening couture... Stroll Calle Ortega y Gasset (Nuñez de Balboa metro stop), and you might find some of the following couturier outposts open late-ish: **Gianni Versace** (tel 577–37–88; #10); **Kenzo** (tel 435–65–93; #11); **Giorgio Armani** (tel 577–37–88; #16); and Madrid's own **Adolfo Domínguez** (tel 576–00–84; #4). Madrid's most exciting homegrown talent may be **Agatha Ruiz de la Prada** (tel 310–44–83; Marqués de Riscal, 8; Rubén Dario metro stop) whose clingy designs feature circus motifs and psychedelic colors. **Glam** (tel 522–80–54; Fuencarral, 35; Gran Vía metro stop) is the club kid/transvestite version of The Limited, purveying mostly secondhand fashionably anti-fashion night-crawler gear, from leather hot pants and sequin shirts to retro sunglasses and glitter boots. **Amor y Cía** (tel 593–08–40; Carranza, 13; Bilbao metro stop) is a treasure trove of kitsch couture from the forties to the eighties, including wild vinyl, rubber, and polyester "threads."

Spanish wares... Madrid is famed for leather and shoes. **Antigua Casa Crespo** (tel 521–56–54; Divino Pastor, 29; San Bernardo metro stop; open Mon–Sat until 8pm) crafts hardy, one-of-a-kind espadrilles. **Loewe** (tel 578–39–21; Serrano, 26; Serrano metro stop; open Mon–Sat until 8:30pm) fashions sensuously supple belts, jackets, suitcases, wallets, and purses for men and women. **Cerámica El Alfar** (tel 411–35–87; Claudio Coello, 112; Nuñez de Balboa metro stop; open Mon–Sat until 9pm) showcases the tiles and pottery of Andalusia and Valencia, in both traditional and strikingly contemporary styles. **Albedrío** (tel 521–50–56; Infantas, 32; Chueca metro stop; open Mon–Sat until 8:30pm) collects the finest crafts, including glass, jewelry, and hand-painted china, from around Spain. **Sobrinas de Pérez** (tel 521–19–54; Postas, 6; Sol metro stop; closed Sat) is a crowded cathedral to gilt iconography, from crèches to candles to crucifixes. **Casa Jiménez** (tel 548–05–26; Preciados, 42; Callao metro stop; closed Sat) specializes in intricate Spanish lace mantillas, embroidered shawls, and tablecloths.

And they're off!... Soccer may be *el deporte rey* ("the king of sports") but what about the "sport of kings"? Only in Madrid would horse racing take a backseat to partying that nightly puts the weeklong Kentucky Derby bash to shame. The races themselves are secondary to the action at the numerous *terrazas* (outdoor restaurants, bars, and discos) ringing the track, filled with *la gente guapa* (beautiful people) dressed like Triple Crown clotheshorses and working-class stiffs belting back a few stiff ones. The action is visible from each *terraza*, and if betting, boogying, and bingeing aren't enough, the ancillary entertainment includes bungee-jumping, bowling, bumper bikes, and bands. The track itself, called **Hipódromo de la Zarzuela** (tel 307–01–40; Carretera de la Coruña, along N-VI at km. 7.8; 500 ptas. per person, more if a concert is scheduled) is open June through September Friday and Saturday 10:30pm to 2am. Though it's outside the city center, free buses labeled "Hipódromo" run to and from the Moncloa subway station regularly between 10:30pm and 1am. Taxis are available for diehards.

For mallrats... Big malls close by 9 or 10pm, even in summer; unlike their stateside counterparts, they attract a settled set barking into their cell phones or chatting at the numerous cafes. You won't find video arcades, fast-food joints, or Disney/Reebok infestations. **Galería del Prado** (tel 429–75–51; Plaza de las Cortes, 7; Banco de España metro stop) is a subterranean village under the luxurious Palace Hotel, with small boutiques specializing in expensive leather, suede, furs, and bijoux; check out Casandra for designer wear from Armani, Moschino, and Gaultier, and Gourmet del Palacio for Spanish gourmet items. **El Jardín de Serrano** (tel 577–00–12; Goya, 6–8, Serrano metro stop) resembles a posh hotel lobby: marble floors, towering potted plants, wicker chairs. Jazz, not muzak, wafts through the space, which offers Bulgari, Cerruti, and YSL. **ABC Serrano** (tel 577–50–31; Serrano, 61; Rubén Darío metro stop) is in a century-old neoclassical structure. The gorgeous exterior features tiles, iron grillwork, and arabesque arches; the modernized interior features a five-story circular atrium. Its shops offer everything from African decorative arts to electronics, as well as sportier designers like Sergio Tacchini. **Centro Comercial Moda** (General Perón, 32–36; Lima metro stop) is Madrid's most high-tech shopping center, with skylights, steel columns, marble floors, a fountain, and Spanish muzak. The stores are primarily middle-of-the-road middle-class: Benetton, Levi's, and Aalto (Finnish housewares).

Killing time between clubs... Madrid has two one-stop-shopping chains. **VIPs** (main branches: tel 577–12–90, Serrano, 41; tel 319–40–65, Miguel Angel, 11; and tel 319–85–88, Zurbano, 26) are 7–11 meets Woolworth's: videos, books, grocery, liquor, snacks, cafeteria, CDs, toys, souvenirs, and panty hose. Most are open 24 hours a day, or at least until 3:30am on weekends. **BOBs** (main branches: tel 521–20–37, Gran Vía, 29; tel 595–62–00, Plaza Callao; tel 575–06–40, Goya, 18; and tel 577–36–74, Serrano, 24) run a close second in the variety department, offering perfume, electronics, cameras (and film developing), videos, records, and of course, a bar. Most branches remain open until at least 1am.

Music of the night... The main branch of **Madrid Rock** (tel 521–02–39; Gran Vía, 25; Gran Vía metro stop; open until 10pm) is music central, with a comprehensive Tower/Virgin Records–style selection, as well as a ticket booth for concerts. The clientele and selection of records (as well as books and magazines) are more bourgeois at the French-owned **FNAC** (tel 595–61–00; Preciados, 28; Callao metro stop; open until 10pm). The Smashing Pumpkin/Marilyn Manson/King Sunny Ade crowds hang at **Mad House Projects** (tel 593–28–47; de la Palma, 3; Tribunal metro stop; open Mon–Sat until 9pm), which stocks an esoteric collection of alternative and ethnic sounds, including zouk, funk, trip-hop, trance, and techno.

Video arcadia... **Metropolitano** (Gran Vía, 69; Gran Vía metro stop) offers two floors of electronic wizardry for the barely legal: video lotto, poker, and 21; sports-related video games like ski races, "virtual" boxing, car racing, cybercycles to race through the city; plus perennials like Mortal Kombat. Downstairs are pool tables (*billar Americano*), foosball, air hockey, and electronic bowling and basketball. **Salon Las Vegas** (corner of Fuencarral and Sagasta; Bilbao metro stop) concentrates on video gambling games and slots for an older, vaguely vagrant crowd.

5

late night
dining

Unless you indulge in the
delightful customs of tapas,
Madrid is not a city for
hypoglycemics or anyone
whose blood chemistry
goes wacko without an
early dinner. Ten at night is

considered unfashionably early for dinner, which normally crawls on until 1am (for which reason, this chapter would be practically unchanged if it focused on regular as oppposed to "late night" dining). Most restaurants don't even open until 9 and they're usually quiet as a chapel at that hour. It gets mighty uncomfortable eating while a tuxedoed waiter, napkin folded crisply over his arm, stands rigidly at attention—a composition as stately and formal as a Velázquez painting.

In addition to tapas bars, there are thousands of restaurants suiting every mood, taste, and pocketbook. Madrid may not boast the culinary U.N. of other international capitals. But it's a splendid place to sample Spain's remarkably varied fare: Spanish cuisine is one of the world's most underrated. Most people think only of paella, that famous Valencian rice casserole. Instead, think of Spain as several different countries, each with its own distinct culture, customs, language, and cuisine.

Among the top regional specialties are Castile's *cocido* (stew of meats, beans, cabbage, chick-peas and noodles) and *cochinillo* (roast suckling pig); Catalonia's rich, sultry *suquet de peix* (a briny broth coaxed from various shellfish and crustaceans); the Basque *bacalao al pil pil* (cod simmered in garlic until its fat and juices congeal into a velvety blanket for the sweet firm flesh); Andalusian *rabo de toro* (braised bull's tail); Asturian *fabada* (white beans, *morcilla* (black sausage), and *chorizo*); and Galician *pulpo a feira* (octopus marinated in salt, olive oil, and peppers) and *caldo gallego* (a hearty ham and vegetable soup).

Restaurant Facts

Reservations are scrupulously honored. But, with the exception of a few cases noted below in The Index, reservations are rarely necessary. The menu of the day (*menú del día*) often represents superior value, but your choice is limited, if not completely set (and at smaller establishments they may be serving you lunch warmed over). The 7 percent IVA is included in the price; service is occasionally included, but tipping (no more than 10 percent) is left to your discretion. Casual but stylish dress is the rule of thumb, save at a few of the gastronomic altars listed below. The typical dinner begins with soup, salad, or entrée (appetizer), then main course, then dessert. There is a 50 ptas. to 200 ptas. surcharge for bread, which is usually brought automatically to your table. If you order bottled water, specify either *con gas* (sparkling) or *sin gas* (clear).

Sherry and Other Spanish Wines and Spirits

The word sherry itself is an English corruption of *jerez*, but in Spain, the golden elixir is most often referred to by type: *fino, manzanilla, amontillado, oloroso,* and *palo cortado. Finos* are pale, frosty blond, and so bone-dry that they may grate on unsuspecting American palates. The complex bouquets and flavors range from green apple and almonds to woodsy truffles and burnt mesquite. *Manzanillas* are an even crisper *fino* from Sanlucar, carrying with them the salt and tang of the sea. *Amontillados* are older *finos*, aged in wood at least eight years until they turn a lustrous gold and acquire a nutty, spicy flavor. *Olorosos* are deep amber or teak in color, lush, fat, and incredibly concentrated, with wonderful spice, walnut, and Brazil nut flavors. The extremely rare *palo cortados* combine the best aspects of *amontillados* and *olorosos*, with colors ranging from pecan to mahogany, and irresistibly exotic overtones of chocolate, coconut, coffee, cinnamon, or dried fruits.

Many of the finest Spanish red wines are produced in La Rioja (northeast of Madrid). The best gran reservas from the Rioja Alta region are at least seven years old. They're silky, rather delicate, and admirably balanced. Among the better *bodegas* (vineyards) are Bilbainas (especially Viña Pomal), CUNE (Imperial), Marqués de Murrieta, Federico Paternina, La Rioja Alta (Reserva 904), and Marqués de Riscal. The Rioja whites are citrusy, perfumed, low-acid, but undistinguished.

The Ribera del Duero region also produces notable reds, including Spain's most expensive wine, Vega Sicilia (worth every penny!). Dueros are masculine wines of both backbone and finesse, with notes of blackberry and briar, comparable to a great Bordeaux. Penedès is known both for its inky and earthy yet fruity reds like Torres Gran Coronas (Black Label is the highest quality), and *cava*, the Spanish version of champagne. While most *cava* is over-oaked and cloying (witness the cheap export labels of Codorniú and Freixenet), many have surprising breeding: lemony, crisp, and as dry as the desert. Try Juvé y Camps and Vallformosa.

Spanish brandies will come as a delightful surprise. They're rich and nutty, with just a hint of sweetness. Top names include Lepanto, Gran Duque de Alba, Carlos I, and Cardenal Mendoza. Finally, there's the local firewater, *aguardiente,* made, like Italian grappa and French marc, from the must (residue) of grapes after pressing. Those from the finest vineyards have incredible concentration of flavor, once you get past the burn.

Chic, cheap, and creative... **Gula Gula** is theatrical in
every sense, starting with its boldly colored tablecloths and
continuing through its fanciful food presentations. The
waiters look as if they used Gaudí as their haberdasher,
wearing faboo festive, formless hats designed by Brazilian
Sergio Ianino. It's strictly a place for light fare—meat and
yucca pie, salads, quiches. The impromptu spectacles are
legendary; they usually feature drag queens, but the owners
have been known to coax pregnant ballerinas to perform,
tutus and all. The tone at **Momo** is established when you
enter: a huge grinning doll holds a hand-painted menu. The
decor and ambience are warm, witty, and whimsical: red
chairs, enormous warped mirrors, carnival masks, a brightly colored mosaic, and glitter sparkling on the walls. The
food is just as entertaining, unorthodox yet surprisingly
successful: cod in lemon mustard sauce, carrot and orange
tart, veal scaloppini with fig sauce, turkey with pistachios,
smoked salmon with cognac and cilantro. The rooftop
terrace of **El Viajero** is the place to be during the summer—tables are booked weeks in advance. It's the closest a
regular restaurant comes to a club in Madrid. Stick to simpler items, the more cholesterol the better. **La Cacharrería**
means junk shop and the amusing decor fits the name: a
huge illuminated linen pipe winding around the space like
a mutant lantern, an enormous dinner bell that could sum-
mon an entire village. The food is similarly imaginative
and, thankfully, well executed: shrimp and pumpkin flan or
rooster filet steamed with mushrooms and a martini. The
mood is as bubbly as the various *cavas* on the wine list at
Champagnería Gala. The lesbian owners have a bit of a
self-righteous attitude, but the muscle-boy and -girl waitstaff is gabby and cute, as is the mixed clientele. The decor
is sunny, with bright yellow walls trimmed with painted

leaves, and an enclosed garden patio. The low prices and high quality would make anyone feel giddy: a three-course menu is only 1,500 ptas. Innovative specials include cod with leeks and clams or rabbit with snails, but the signature dish is the intriguing Catalan variation on paella called *fideuá*, which utilizes noodles instead of rice. The traditional look—wood tables and bar, lace curtains, abstract artwork, and provocative photos—of **La Chocolatería** belies the unconventional menu and clientele (transvestites to Trotskyites). The inventive and mostly vegetarian and seafood menu includes tasty onion pie with leek and carrot mousse, silky salmon "pudding," and prawns stroganoff. **La Vaca Verónica** is a cheerful place, with bright yellow and flamingo-pink walls contrasting with naughty black lace curtains resembling lingerie. The uncomplicated yet appealing dishes include spaghetti with smoked salmon and caviar or dolphinfish baked in salt. The name means Veronica the Cow, and there are numerous explanatory anecdotes; depending on which staff member you ask, it refers either to the owners once-favorite pet heifer, or to a regular customer.

Institutions... **Lhardy** opened its oak doors in 1839 and seems frozen in the Romantic era; you half expect to find a bewigged and stockinged waitstaff. It's a bastion of neoclassicism, from the opulent decor—pressed walls, gas lamp chandeliers, red velour, lace, chinoiserie, gilt, and private salons—to the sumptuous food—pheasant with grapes, stewed partridge, venison, hake with baby eels, sea bass with giant prawns, roast veal Orloff. **Restaurant Goya** lives up to the rigorous standards of the Hotel Ritz. Tapestries, marble columns and hand-embroidered linens bespeak its status. Huge picture windows overlook a charming garden (where a lighter, more casual menu is served in summer) with white wicker chairs, lily pond, and flowing fountains. The seasonal menu emphasizes specialties from around Spain. **Horcher** defines institution: a plush setting, sterling silver service and fussy but phenomenal cooking (from game, like partridge and wild duck casserole, to humbler Central European specialties like goulash and sauerbraten). Rumor has it that **Botín** was to Hemingway what Cheers was to Norm Peterson; Goya washed dishes here. This venerable eatery is a warren of rooms on four floors of ancient beams, tiled floors, stone walls, wood-burning ovens, and pots and pans dangling everywhere. The kitchen excels in hearty roast meats, preparing the definitive *cochinillo* (roast suckling pig) and *cordero asado* (roast lamb). No surprise that **La Trainera** is one of Madrid's foremost seafood houses—the owner was a fish wholesaler before becoming a restaurateur. The marvelous fish is delicate and flaky, never overcooked, the clams and oysters are fresh and briny as can be, and you can even choose your own lobster from the tank. The nautical decor thankfully stops just short of being obnoxious.

For the tourist trade... **Botín** is the world's oldest continuously operating eatery (opened in 1725—and listed in *The Guinness Book of World Records*). Yes, it's romantic..., unless your fellow diners are somebody's Aunt Louise poking waiters and asking, "Are you sure Hemingway ate at this table?" Models of decorum, the waiters don't even roll their eyes. **Las Cuevas de Luís Candelas** is total tourist kitsch and they eat it up, from the half-baked decor to the overcooked food. Candelas was a famous 19th-century gentleman bandit; the overdressed waiters in period costume try to duplicate his sexy swagger, kissing the hand of every woman who walks in. The decor is both gorgeous and hokey in its sheer extravagance. Despite the hordes of nouveaux riches Germans and British pensioners, plenty of locals still heave understandably orgasmic sighs over the *cocido* at **La Bola**, as if it were their last meal before they meet their maker, or their first food in days. It starts with the stock, poured with an exaggerated flourish from an earthenware jar over a plate of noodles and beans. Then chickpeas and cabbage, and finally the meats are served. There are a few organ meats Americans would prefer not to know about. You'd swear **Casa Santa Cruz** was a stop on a tour-group itinerary, the way diners "ooh" and "ahh." Originally a chapel (the domed ceiling is impressive with its gold gilt and frescoes), it also served as Madrid's first Stock Exchange. No one could be bullish about the high prices for good but standard dishes like roast lamb. Nonetheless, the reverent waitstaff presents everything with fulsome fanfare, as if they expect you to break out in the Hallelujah Chorus.

Too cool for their own good... Madrid is packed with

yuppetteries which can be enjoyed for their sheer extravagance as well as mostly fine food. The PYTs (Pretty Young Things) packing the three floors of tiny pink rooms at **Palacio de Anglona** are as drop-dead (and judging from the meet-and-greet scene between couples, just as incestuous) as the "Melrose Place" bunch. One Madrid wag dubs it the place "where sexy but cheap would-be actors and models go for cheap but sexy food." Hemingway would have roared in agony at the painfully popular **Geographic Club.** The decorators were hell-bent on living up to the name, with a "one-from-column-A" approach: treasure maps; bear rugs; masks from Polynesia, Africa, South America; sailing ship models; Zulu spears; fertility god icons from Celebes; "neoclassical" Bacchus and Athena statues; a Chinese gong; painted Hindu screens; a mini-replica of an old-style safari jeep; the obligatory trophy heads; and displays of "typical Indonesian cannibal garb." The menu offers simple fare like good ol'-fashioned "Kenya burgers" (really just a glorified beef patty). **Samarkanda** is the most bombastic restaurant in town. The menu out-nouvelles nouvelle with its artfully arranged, infinitesimal portions of ordinary dishes like beef tournedos with stuffed tomatoes; better hope your eyes are bigger than your stomach. Converted from the unused part of the old railway station, it's rigged to resemble a tropical colonial outpost with an oddly British rather than Spanish flavor. The pompous **Pedro Larumbe** might be accused of feeling its hautes. The interior, classified as a historic-artistic monument, is almost absurdly flamboyant Art Nouveau. The pretentiousness extends to the admittedly first-rate food, which the chef labels *cocina de autor* (cuisine of the auteur, with added hauteur); two of the more successful entries are hake rolled with shrimp, or skate Vizcaína made with red pepper and onion sauce. On the plus side, the terrace has a splendid view of the Castellana.

For carnivores... **Chicago's** advertises "the best American ribs" in town (but Memphis it ain't). Neon beer signs, loud music (live rock on weekends), louder conversation, brick walls, Dick Tracy cartoons in Spanish, and gangster statuary (Al Capone and Dillinger). In other words, typically American. At least that's how Europeans see it, which is a frightening thought. Appropriately enough, it's situated across the street from its inspiration, the **Hard Rock Café**. You know the drill: posters of The Who, Queen, Beastie Boys; blaring music videos; platinum records from New Kids on the Block and the Commodores; guitars from Gene Simmons, Stevie Ray Vaughan, and ZZ Top (who must have a merchandising deal). The handsome wood and stained-glass bar is a predictably popular hangout with tourists and local yuppies alike. At least the burgers are good—hefty heifers dripping with juice and perfectly charred. **Beef Place** imports its meat from Argentina. Its polished wood floors, green tile-and-faux-stone walls, and comely abstract paintings counter the unassuming Sizzler's exterior. You order the dry-aged beef by weight—baby, super, extra, and big; the entrecôte, filet mignon, and free-range beef are just as mouth-watering. Dripping with authenticity, **El Buey** ("the ox") is famed for its delicious sizzling steak tenderloin platter, *lomo de buey,* truly a feast for all five senses. The room is all gleaming wood, bullfight posters, and red-and-white-checked cloths.

Gastronomic temples... The cooking at **Viridiana** is as individualistic, as shocking, as Buñuel's films. The dazzling juxtapositions of taste, color, texture, and scent include shrimp crepes with baby asparagus, duck-liver brioche in sauternes, blinis with snail and *romesco* (red pepper, almond, and garlic dip), veal scaloppini rolled with blue cheese and snow peas, ox sirloin with white and black truffles and foie gras, and mascarpone pastry with marsala and white chocolate. Even the presentation is playful: Rabbit and venison are entwined with greens to re-create a forest scene of writhing snakes and browning leaves. They take wine seriously, though, even decanting younger reds by candlelight the old-fashioned way. The extraordinary list is not only comprehensive, but fairly priced. The contemporary space is austere yet warm: black, gray, and white with clever canary accents, willow vases, recessed lamps, and stills of Buñuel films lining the walls just above an eye-level strip of mirrors (for discreet narcissism). The downstairs sports a more romantic look, with brick walls and photos. The crowd is mixed: rock stars in leather and vinyl, Almodóvar, English and American celebs from the Ritz just a few blocks away. Yet there's magically no attitude, not even from the waitstaff.

LATE NIGHT DINING ◊ THE LOWDOWN

Owner-chef Tomás Herranz recently lowered his prices but not his standards at the venerable **El Cenador del Prado**. The food is incredibly creative; witness grilled salmon in cumin sauce, venison medallions drizzled with raspberry vinaigrette, shellfish in cream sauce with mussel *empanadillas* (pastries), shrimp and green-bean ravioli in sweet-and-sour sauce, and duck thigh in caramel. At 3,500 ptas. the tasting menu (menu *degustación*) is a remarkable bargain. The interior design is as hedonistic as the menu, all gold and crimson amid a virtual greenhouse of lush exotic plants. **Zalacaín** offers not just a memorable meal but an experience to be savored, from the *amuses-gueules* presented when you're seated (perhaps a thimbleful of velvety mushroom shrimp bisque or potato croquettes) to the petits fours after dinner. Transcendent appetizers include lukewarm pheasant salad with wild mushrooms, oysters with caviar and sherry jelly, and truffle lasagna with foie gras. For an entree choose from heavenly duck stew, artichoke-stuffed prawns, or fresh goose-liver blinis in old Rioja. Finish with chocolate mint sorbet or a trilogy of tea-based custards with raspberry, lemon, and chocolate flavorings. The three dining rooms are imposing yet not ostentatious. An aura of well-deserved self-congratulation surrounds the peerless waitstaff (neither fawning nor feigning, murmuring "excellent choice" no matter what without seeming obsequious). Guests all wear corporate drag, even on Saturday; you'd think they came straight from the office (they probably did). Everything at **Gastroteca de Stephane y Arturo**, from the welcome to the food, is stylish and a tad eccentric. Stephane Guérin, the chef, and her husband, Arturo, the meeter and greeter, offer more than just a gastronomic experience. They liken dining to relaxation techniques, with soothing New Age music, candlelight creating intriguing shadows over the space's DeChiricoesque clean lines, and flowers and potpourri providing aromatherapy. Stephane believes that different foods induce different psychological states; no psychedelic mushrooms here, but diners' moods usually border on the ecstatic. Such singular creations as black-olive sorbet and skate with ginger and vanilla guarantee nostalgic reminiscences.

Best regional Spanish... **La Barraca** is the palace of paella: try the traditional *Valenciana* (chicken, rabbit, veggies), *marinera* (mussels, shrimps, prawns, squid, halibut), or a *mixta* of the two. The restaurant's name is quite a pun: a *barraca* is a hut or shack, but the decor here is closer to Baroque. The grand rooms are cluttered with every imaginable kind of hand-painted china hanging on walls, dangling from ceilings, posing proudly in cabinets, as if several Valencian grandmothers had emptied their attics. Even the chandeliers are porcelain. The large collection of musketry is thoroughly incongruous in the otherwise dainty surroundings. **Viuda de Vacas** is a less-touristy, attitude-free typical Madrid tavern, with tiles, wood beams, mahogany bar, red-and-white-checked tablecloths, and an iron spiral staircase leading to the kitchen and a second dining room. The wondrous food is culled from northern Spain: cod stew, quail stuffed with foie gras and mushrooms, and the famous specialty, *pimientos del padrón*—a mix of fried peppers, some hot, some not, the gastronomic equivalent of Russian roulette. **La Bodeguita del Caco** means "thieves' den," and you can get thick as thieves in this romantic, old-fashioned space, decorated with *porrones* (ceramic jars), charming miniature paintings, tiny guitars, leaded glass, and brass chandeliers. The inexpensive Canary Islands fare draws upon a rich stew pot of Spanish culinary traditions and African ingredients: specialties include *sama a la sal* (a delicate sweet fish baked in salt), *puchero Canario* (chickpeas, pears, yams, carrots, pork, and ham stew so lusciously thick that it seems to have been bubbling for days), rabbit in *salmorejo* (a gazpacho-like combination of tomatoes, peppers, onions, and garlic), and beef medallions in onion and honey sauce. There are also delectable, gastronomically related Caribbean dishes like fish with coconut and *chicharrones de pollo* (spiced chicken fingers). **O'Pazo** flies its seafood in fresh from Galicia every day. Try monkfish in green sauce, *vieiras* (the local version of coquilles St. Jacques), or *empanadas de lampreas* (pastries stuffed with ground lamprey eel). If you'd rather put meat on your bones, order the *caldo gallego* or *lacon con grelos* (sort of Galician corned beef and cabbage). The restaurant is large, well-lit, and bustling, with funny Sardi-style caricatures of famous diners, pink napery, and brass everywhere. **Cabo Mayor** celebrates the food of Cantabria (a northern coastal province). The seafood is suitably excellent (try the grilled hake in wild mushroom sauce or sea bass and potato casserole), the decor contemporary marine (blue tile floors, model ships, miniature sail rigging), and the largely fat-cat business clientele whale-bellied and blowhard. The cavernous, 1910 cider house and student haunt **Casa Mingo** specializes in the plain, hearty food of mountainous, impoverished Asturias; the cider packs a surprising wallop, and makes a superb baste for the tender spit-roasted chicken and fried chorizos. **Gure Etxea** excels in Basque preparations like *huevos revueltos* (scrambled eggs) with spinach and shellfish, *bacalao al pil pil,* (see introduction) and a true delicacy (when they're available), *anguilas* (tiny crunchy baby eels). The decor is archetypal: wood beams, stucco and brick walls, Basque farm instruments, leaded glass windows, and lace curtains. Catalan cuisine contends with Basque for best of the best in Spain, and **Pedralbes** offers ample proof that the competition's still going strong. Among the scrumptious Catalan dishes served up here are braised rabbit, *pollo de xamfaina* (with eggplant, tomatoes, and peppers), or bull's tail stuffed with fried potatoes. Ecru brickwork, green wicker chairs, Catalan landscapes (nothing with melting watches, though), and dressy, older couples contribute to the classy atmosphere.

Mexican and beyond... At least the garish **Sí Señor** has a sense of humor. The facade is fronted by a bright orange and green plastic palm tree, which serves as an apt metaphor for the antics within. The atmosphere is toga-party rowdy; order a "slam shot" of tequila and they cutely give you a hard hat. The brick-walled interior is a museum of faux Mexican memorabilia: serapes, basketry, life-sized dolls in ponchos, forties Mexican B movie posters, and truly hideous paintings of honest Mexican "laborers." Given that, it's still Madrid's best "South of the Border" spot, with chicken molé consistently garnering olés. It's criminal what they've done to the lovely old building off the Plaza Mayor that houses **El Cuchi**: the original wood beams and tiling compete with the T-shirts for sale, a frieze of skeletons strumming guitars, and a neon sign proclaiming this the "Museum of Beer" (in English, no less, which gives you a clue about the clientele). They offer an encyclopedic collection of beers from around the world, as well as margaritas in rainbow colors. The food, too, is what you'd expect—enchiladas, chiles rellenos, etc. The great Cuban salsa singer Celia Cruz owns the jumping **Zara**, which serves up predictably potent *mojitos*. It's quite pretty, with stained glass, red tile roof, stucco walls, and red-and-white tablecloths. The food is comparatively indifferent: safe bets include roast veal, a wide range of omelettes (from banana to tuna to sausage), and *arroz con pollo* (chicken with rice).

Eastern fare with flair... **Al-Mounia** resembles a posh pasha's digs, with opulent Mudejar tiles and arches, intricate mosaic work, and big cushy pillows to lounge on. The food is divine, including classic couscous, *pastillas* (pigeon pie), and *tajines.* To burn off the calories, try mimicking the sultry belly dancers, who have astounding abdominal control. **Dinasty** is haute Chinese in every respect. The sleek contemporary decor includes a reproduction of a Ming emperor's robe, huge painted fans, and high-back black lacquer chairs that anyone but a chiropractor would find uncomfortable. The waitresses glide gracefully about as if they were in the Forbidden Palace. The food, while hardly original by American standards, is sublimely prepared; specialties include hake medallions in soy and ginger, Peking duck, beef rolled with wild mushrooms, and sweet-and-sour shrimp. **Donzoko** is a favorite of local Japanese businesspeople (always a good sign). The sushi is remarkably tasty and practically jumps on your plate, the tempura feathery light. The waitresses pad about as silently as spies, befitting the zen-like, meditative atmosphere, which is enhanced by a little interior rock garden and bamboo booths.

Pasta, pizza, etc.... **L'Arrabbiata** is certainly a sexy space for a shopping center eatery, and faux brickwork contrasts surrealistically with brightly painted walls and huge brass supports. It serves more than adequate Italian dishes like spaghetti with clam sauce and *tagliatelle mar e monti* (chicken, rabbit, beef). But its real claim to fame are the "opera nights" (Thur–Sat), when staff members dress up like hip matadors in shiny vinyl jackets (the audience sometimes dresses to match). The tenors and sopranos are game but quavery. **La Alpargatería** means shoe shop, and the owner's ancestors were indeed cobblers. The reasonably priced, flavorful, perfectly al dente pastas (go for any of the ravioli specials) click with the well-heeled clientele. The quietly elegant space resembles a tony Tuscan cottage: straw lamps, brick walls, cushy banquettes, indoor trellises. The savory, clever pizzas at **La Gata Flora** include Roquefort, octopus, and puttanesca. The pastas are more standard, running toward bolognese, carbonara, and pesto. The restaurant is very pretty: coral and lavender walls, arches, and the requisite red-and-white checked tablecloths, with chic spotlighting illuminating an eclectic crowd from bikers and their babes to heavy metal rockers.

For Wheeler Dealers... A quietly powerful older crowd, from actors and their producers to political seers and CEOs, holds court at **Casa Lucio**. The interior is imposing yet homey: traditional brick arches, wood beams, red tablecloths, Sevillan porcelain, and pots and pans. Power-brokering stops when the scrumptious food arrives. Try the succulent roast lamb or pheasant with beans. After dinner, everyone looks perfectly at home with their cognacs and cigars. Up-and-coming sharks and young-bloods favor **Julián de Tolosa**, just across the street. The soaring duplex space is cool, attractive, smart but not smart-ass, with dramatic lighting, brick walls, modernist chairs and tables, enormous earthenware pots that look like they could be used to bury mummies, and polished wood floors. The menu is simple, running toward hake in garlic sauce with green beans or luscious veal chops. **La Ancha** sees a sea of suits currying favors from members of Parliament. Despite the romantic ambience and decor—oak, etched glass, crystal chandeliers—the top-secret deals negotiated in the luxe private salons are affairs of state, not the prelude to a state of undress. The menu features deftly prepared standards like grilled hake or sole, garlic shrimp, and roast lamb. Ultra-chic **Iroco**, a hangout of Almodóvar and his groupies, lures a picky pijo and professional crowd infected with affluenza. The space is coldly modern but comfortable, the food inventive but a bit ambitious: hake in squid ink, sea bass roasted with garlic confit, artichokes stuffed with eggplant and figs.

$$$$	over 7,500 ptas.	more than $60
$$$	4,500–7,500 ptas.	$35–$60
$$	2,500–4,500 ptas.	$20–$35
$	under 2,500 ptas.	Less than $20

Prices reflect average price for three courses per person; service included; drinks are not included.

La Alpargatería. Fine, inexpensive, yet atmospheric Italian, popular with an older, successful crowd.... *Tel 577–43–45. Hermosilla, 7; Serrano metro stop. DC not accepted. $$*
(see p. 111)

Al-Mounia. The prices at this exquisitely decorated, ultra-chic Moroccan would make a sheik shriek.... *Tel 435–08–28. Recoletos, 5; Banco de España metro stop. Closed Sun, Mon, Aug. DC not accepted. $$–$$$* **(see p. 111)**

La Ancha. Traditional dishes appeal to a tradition-bound power clientele.... *Tel 49–81–86. Zorrilla, 7; Banco de España metro stop. Closed Sun. DC not accepted. $$–$$$*
(see p. 112)

La Barraca. Despite the extensive menu, paella is the only thing to order at this amazingly over-decorated space, popular for nearly a half-century.... *Tel 532–71–54. Reina, 29; Gran Vía metro stop. DC not accepted. $$* **(see p. 109)**

Beef Place. The name says it all, although you'll also find near-classic onion soup, creditable Caesar salad.... *Tel 556–41–87. Avda. Brasil, 30; Cuzco metro stop. DC not accepted. $$* **(see p. 107)**

La Bodeguita del Caco. Canarian charmer with exotic cuisine for folks with large appetites and small pockets.... *Tel 429–40–23. Echegaray, 27; Antón Martín metro stop. Closed Mon. No credit cards. $–$$* **(see p. 109)**

La Bola. Stereotypically quaint turn-of-the-century Madrid standby where burping is almost mandatory after gorging on the glorious *cocido*, a meal in itself.... *Tel 547–69–30. Bola, 5; Santo Domingo metro stop. Closed Sun. No credit cards. $$* **(see p. 105)**

Botín. Everybody who's anyone and thousands who aren't have sampled the superb grilled meats and the historic ambience.... *Tel 366–42–17. Cuchilleros, 17; Sol metro stop. Reservations recommended. $$–$$$* **(see pp. 104, 105)**

El Buey. As warm and welcoming as the eponymous steak specialty: *lomo de buey*.... *Tel 431–44–92. General Pardiñas, 10; Goya metro stop. DC not accepted. $$* **(see p. 107)**

Cabo Mayor. Fine regional seafood restaurants, with sleek look and slick clientele.... *Tel 350–87–76. Juan Ramón Jiménez, 37; Cuzco metro stop. Reservations recommended. Closed Sun. $$–$$$* **(see p. 109)**

La Cacharrería. Good offbeat choice thanks to Dalíesque decor, hip young crowd, low prices.... *Tel 365–39–30. Morería, 9; La Latina metro stop. Closed Sun. $$* **(see p. 103)**

Casa Lucio. Rustic elegant Madrid tavern attracting the see-and-be-scene herd.... *Tel 365–32–52. Cava Baja, 35; La Latina metro stop. Reservations recommended. $$$* **(see p. 112)**

Casa Mingo. Known for its simple roasts and bustling *terraza*.... *Tel 547–79–18. Paseo de la Florida, 2; Príncipe Pío metro stop. Closed Aug. No credit cards. $* **(see p. 110)**

Casa Santa Cruz. Overpriced, yet not overrated, as the mouth-watering food almost matches the eye-catching ex-church decor.... *Tel 521–86–23. De la Bolsa, 12; Sol metro stop. $$$* **(see p. 105)**

El Cenador del Prado. The scintillating bill of fare at this sumptuous restaurant is presented at a fair bill.... *Tel 429–15–61. Prado, 4; Sevilla metro stop. Reservations required. $$–$$$* **(see p. 108)**

Champagnería Gala. As festive as the name suggests, offering penthouse food and atmosphere at bargain basement prices.... *Tel 429–26–62. Moratín, 22; Antón Martín metro stop. Restaurant closed all day Thur, Sat night (bar open). No credit cards. $–$$* **(see p. 103)**

Chicago's. A burger and beers joint, with fancy-schmancy decor, live rock, and madrileños eating it up.... *Tel 577–52–39. Paseo de la Castellana, 4; Colón metro stop. DC not accepted. $–$$* **(see p. 106)**

La Chocolatería. A very trendy crowd enjoys the inexpensive, original dishes until fairly late in the evening.... *Tel 521–00–23. Barbieri, 15; Chueca metro stop. No credit cards. $–$$* **(see p. 104)**

El Cuchi. Clichéd Mexican fare absorbs the alcohol at this party-hearty tourist joint.... *Tel 366–44–24. Cuchilleros, 3; Sol metro stop. Closed Sun. DC not accepted. $–$$*

(see p. 110)

Las Cuevas de Luís Candelas. Twice the price for the same food as at nearby restaurants that are just as "atmospheric," just as "authentic." But everything is so hilariously overdone, this clip joint's almost worth it.... *Tel 366–54–28. Cuchilleros, 1; Sol metro stop. $$$* **(see p. 105)**

Dinasty. The kind of posh Chinese where you have to pay for your rice on the side, but it's Madrid's best.... *Tel 431–08–47. O'Donnell, 31; Príncipe de Vergara metro stop. DC not accepted. $$* **(see p. 111)**

Donzoko. Tranquil oasis amid the hubbub of the Santa Ana area serving appetizing Japanese food at even tastier prices.... *Tel 429–57–20. Echegaray, 3; Sevilla metro stop. Closed Sun. DC not accepted. $$* **(see p. 111)**

Gastroteca de Stephane y Arturo. A fascinating place indeed, with smashing food and unusual owners.... *Tel 532–35–64. Plaza de Chueca, 8; Chueca metro stop.*

Reservations recommended. Closed Sun. $$$
(see p. 108)

La Gata Flora. Cute, gussied-up pizza joint makes an amusing contrast to its grungy Malasaña surroundings (including a heavy-duty biker shop across the street).... *Tel 521–27–92. San Vicente Ferrer, 33; Tribunal metro stop. $***(see p. 112)**

Geographic Club. This shrine to the adventurer in us all may be the next best thing to going on safari, but the yuppie clientele is more bore than wild boar.... *Tel 578–08–62. Alcala, 141; Goya metro stop. DC not accepted. $$*
(see p. 106)

Gula Gula. *Gula* means glutton, but the competent food takes a backseat to the colorful decor, staff, and clientele.... *Tel 420–29–19. Infante, 5; Antón Martín metro stop. DC not accepted. $***(see p. 103)**

Gure Etxea. Spaniards usually concede the Basques are the best chefs. This charming, Old World restaurant confirms it.... *Tel 365–61–49. Plaza de la Paja, 12; La Latina metro stop. Closed Sun. $$–$$$***(see p. 110)**

Hard Rock Café. Same pressing, same label as every other Hard Rock franchise, right down to the T-shirt concession.... *Tel 435–02–00. Paseo de la Castellana, 2; Colón metro stop. $***(see p. 107)**

Horcher. The namesake German family has operated this stodgy mainstay (jacket and tie still required) for over half a century.... *Tel 532–35–96. Alfonso XII, 6; Retiro metro stop. Reservations required. Closed Sun. $$$$***(see p. 104)**

Iroco. The rooms are airy and contemporary, just like the nouvelle cuisine.... *Tel 431–73–81. Velázquez, 18; Velázquez metro stop. DC not accepted. $$***(see p. 112)**

Julián de Tolosa. Yuppified take on an old Madrid tavern, with clever variations on both traditional decor and food.... *Tel 365–82–10. Cava Baja, 18; La Latina metro stop. DC not accepted. Closed Sun. $$$***(see p. 112)**

L'Arrabbiata. Chic Italian hangout known for its singing waiters.... *Tel 556–90–46. General Perón, 40, C.C. Moda Shopping; Lima metro stop. $–$$* **(see p. 111)**

Lhardy. Over 150 years old and steeped in tradition, with gourmet Continental cuisine to match.... *Tel 522–22–07. Carrera de San Jerónimo, 8; Sol metro stop. Reservations required. Closed Sun. $$$* **(see p. 104)**

Momo. Everything here is wild, wacky, fun, and festive—the decor, the food, and the mixed gay/straight clientele.... *Tel 532–71–62. Augusto Figueroa, 41; Chueca metro stop. No credit cards. $$* **(see p. 103)**

O'Pazo. Fancy business district restaurant patronized primarily by locals.... *Tel 533–23–33. Reina Mercedes, 20; Nuevos Ministerios metro stop. Closed Mon. $$$*

(see p. 109)

Palacio de Anglona. Stays open until 3am, with crowds veering dramatically from yuppie to clubbie, who think they've seen (and eaten) it all.... *Tel 366–37–53. Segovia, 13; La Latina metro stop. DC not accepted. $$* **(see p. 106)**

Pedralbes. In the commercial district and dead at night, but perhaps the best Catalan menu in Madrid.... *Tel 555–30–27. Basílica, 15–17; Nuevos Ministerios metro stop. Closed Sun evening. DC, M not accepted. $$* **(see p. 110)**

Pedro Larumbe. Nouvelle Basque/French/Cantabrian food and decor not merely awash but drowning in fin de siècle splendor.... *Tel 575–11–12. Serrano, 6; Rubén Darió metro stop. Closed Sun. DC not accepted. $$$* **(see p. 106)**

Restaurant Goya. Like dining in a palace, with impeccable service, textbook food, beautiful people of all ages.... *Tel 521–28–57. Hotel Ritz, Plaza de la Lealtad, 5; Banco de España metro stop. Reservations required. $$$$*

(see p. 104)

Samarkanda. Glorious if over-the-top setting isn't worth the exorbitant prices, attitude, and ho-hum food.... *Tel 530–97–46. Estación de Atocha, Glorieta de Carlos V; Atocha metro stop. DC not accepted. $$* **(see p. 106)**

LATE NIGHT DINING ☽ INDEX

Sí Señor. Raucous, fun, gaudy, dangerously stereotypical Mexican with surprisingly acceptable food.... *Tel 564–06–04. Paseo de la Castellana, 128; Lima metro stop. AE, DC not accepted. $–$$* **(see p. 110)**

La Trainera. Bankers, brokers, policy makers frequent this superlative seafood restaurant in ritzy Salamanca.... *Tel 576–05–75. Lagasca, 60; Serrano metro stop. Closed Sun., Aug. DC not accepted. $$–$$$* **(see p. 105)**

La Vaca Verónica. The decor and food are as playful as the name (Veronica the Cow).... *Tel 429–78–27. Moratín, 38; Antón Martín metro stop. Closed Sat lunch, Sun. No credit cards. $–$$* **(see p. 104)**

El Viajero. Pizzas, pastas, pool tables, pop music, eye-popping terrace views at this hot hangout.... *Tel 366–90–64. Plaza de la Cebada, 11; La Latina metro stop. Reservations recommended. Closed Mon. $–$$* **(see p. 103)**

Viridiana. Casual but elegant darling of the foodie firmament. The menu is miraculous, the decor divine, the service saintly.... *Tel 531–52–22. Juan de Mena, 14; Retiro metro stop. Closed Sun. Reservations recommended. $$$–$$$$* **(see p. 107)**

Viuda de Vacas. Traditional Madrid *mesón* (inn), dating back to the turn of the century.... *Tel 366–58–47. Cava Alta, 23; La Latina metro stop. Closed Aug. DC not accepted. $$* **(see p. 109)**

Zalacaín. OK, so jacket and tie are still required, but the staff, right down to the busboys and dishwashers, could write the book on how to run a gourmet establishment.... *Tel 561–59–35. Alvarez de Baena, 4; Ruben Darío metro stop. Reservations required. Closed Sun. $$$$* **(see p. 108)**

Zara. Boisterous, bouncy Cuban restaurant loved more for its drinks than its food.... *Tel 532–20–74. Infantas, 5; Gran Vía metro stop. Closed Sat, Sun, Aug. $–$$* **(see p. 111)**

down
and
dirty

Airports... If you arrive at Madrid's **Barajas International Airport** (tel 305–833–433, 4, or 5) at the crack of dawn, you might feel the whole experience is comparable to being grilled by Torquemada during the Inquisition. Shuttle buses idle in the middle of the tarmac—as patient, if not as orderly, as vultures—waiting to transport unwary, weary passengers to Customs and Immigration. Once they achieve maximum weight load, the drivers set out for the gate with a vengeance, swerving and screeching around each other like bumper cars.

Immigration is usually just a formality, though agents do often hold up the lines, not to question suspected drug lords necessarily, but to chat up acquaintances. The worst wait is for your luggage: the conveyor belts are so worn they resemble slashed tires. Fortunately, however, the arrivals lobby is clean and intelligently laid out, with everything, including information booth, currency exchange, and car-rental desks, in clear view.

Major airlines with daily nonstop service from New York and Miami include **American** (tel 597–20–68), **British Airways** (tel 431–75–75), **Iberia** (tel 329–43–53), and **TWA** (tel 310–30–94).

Airport transportation... Barajas International Airport is 5 kilometers (8 miles) east of Madrid on highway A2, which leads to Avenida de América and to the center city. **Autobús del Aeropuerto** stops underground at the Plaza de Colón, where you can switch to the metro or a taxi (it's about 500–600 ptas. for a taxi ride to the major hotels). Buses run from the airport between 5:15am and 2am daily and from Plaza de Colón between 4:45am and 2:45am, departing roughly every 10 minutes between 7am and 10pm, every 20 minutes at other times. The fare is 350 ptas. Unless you hit heavy traffic, taxi rides between the airport and most major hotels cost around 2,500 ptas. (this includes an automatic 350-ptas. airport-trip surcharge). There are additional surcharges of 50 ptas. for each bag stowed in the trunk, and 150 ptas. if you're riding between 11pm and 6am or on Sunday. Only use taxis from the official ranks outside the airport terminals; Madrid "gypsy" cabbies are notorious for taking the "scenic" route instead of hopping right onto the highway.

All-night pharmacies... Maybe it's a rotating concession. Maybe it's just some uniquely Spanish concept of justice. Whatever it is, the list of pharmacies that stay open around the clock seems to change from week to week. Fortunately, there's generally at least one open in each major neighborhood, and all three of the major papers (*El País, El Mundo,* and *ABC*) carry daily listings, so you shouldn't get much of a headache trying to find one. Also, most pharmacies post a list of their all-night brethren. If it's just pain relievers or the pink stuff you're after, you can always head to one of the 24-hour **VIPs** convenience stores (see Hanging Out).

Babysitting... Considering how much Spain reveres the family, you'd think Madrid would have babysitting agencies. But maybe they're not needed, since families normally dine out together, and there are usually enough relatives along to look after the *niños.* Most hotels, however, do keep a file of reputable sitters on hand. If that doesn't work, another good source of reliable babysitters is the **Centro Infantil Nenos**.

Car rentals... You must be joking. The only conceivable reason for renting a car here is to explore the surrounding countryside; even then it's best to spend the night in worthwhile towns like Toledo, Segovia, Chinchón, or Avila and then sneak back into Madrid between 3am (by which time most revelers have gone home) and 7am (when the rush hour begins for those who either didn't party—or haven't gone home yet). Most of the locals drive like maniacs and honk their horns at the slightest provocation (and given the frequent traffic jams that make L.A.'s freeways seem like cruiser's nirvana, there are *plenty* of provocations). It's also almost impossible to find a parking space on the narrow, crooked side streets; what's more, the parking regulations are Byzantine, and the traffic cops keep an eagle eye out for violators. If you must rent anything, go for a scooter or motorcycle (the preferred wheels for the young, hip, and indigent).

The two most reliable companies, both of which have airport branches and offer substantial weekly discounts, are **Eurodollar-Atesa** (main number, tel 561–48–00; airport, tel 305–86–60; free reservations, tel 902–100–101) and **Europcar** (main number, tel 721–12–22; airport, tel 305–44–20; free reservations, tel 901–102–020). You must be over 21, and a credit card is required for the deposit. Ask whether the rate includes insurance, unlimited mileage, and IVA (the 16% tax). For scooters and motorcycles, try **Motoalquiler** (tel 542–06–57).

Credit cards... For credit-card emergencies, 24 hours a day, call: **American Express** (tel 572–03–20); **MasterCard** (toll-free tel 900/971–231); or **Visa** (toll-free tel 900/974–445). None have offices open at night.

Emergencies... To report crimes, call the **Policía Nacional** at **091**; the main station is centrally located near the Plaza de España at Calle Fomento, 24. Few officers speak English, however, and the red tape is even stickier than in the States. To reach the free **Red Cross** ambulance service, dial **061/522–22–22.** The two central hospitals are **Ciudad Sanitaria La Paz** (tel 358–28–31; Paseo de la Castellana, 261; metro Begoña), which is the largest, and **Hospital General Gregorio Marañón** (tel 586–80–00; Doctor Esquerdo, 46; metro Ibiza or O'Donnell), which accepts patients without medical insurance. For minor ailments , you can head to one of the around-the-clock first-aid centers called **Casas de Socorro** (central: tel 521–00–25; Navas de Tolosa, 10; metro Callao).

The **American Embassy** (tel 577–40–00; Serrano, 75) is open limited hours during the day and, unless you know the ambassador's private line, an answering service will direct you to call back during regular hours.

Festivals and special events... Consult the *Guía del Ocio* for specific times and places.

February: **ARCO** (tel 722–50–00; Feria de Madrid/IFEMA, Parque Ferial Juan Carlos I; metro Arturo Soria connecting to bus 122), is an enormous gathering of artists and gallery owners, purporting to present the world's most avant-garde artworks in a variety of media; it's billed like the Whitney Biennial or the Venice Biennale, but it's really more like a Vegas convention. The Fundación Caja de Madrid presents a top-notch **Festival de Flamenco** (tel 521–30–88). Madrid's **Carnaval** hardly rivals those in Rio, Trinidad, or the Big Easy for sheer extravagance, but certain neighborhoods outdo themselves in drinking, dancing, and dressing up (especially the flamboyant parades and parties in the streets of Chueca, the gay barrio). The festivities culminate on Ash Wednesday afternoon with the peculiar *Entierro de la Sardina* (Interment of the Sardine), when thousands of people and several jazz bands accompany a sardine in a small casket on a long march all over town, before burying the little fella with great fanfare on the Paseo de la Florida. The fish is a symbol of early Christianity, and the beginning of fasting.

March: **La Semana de la Mujer,** the week surrounding March 8, International Women's Day, is marked by a parade, various fiestas in bars, and cultural events celebrating women's achievements. **La Semana Santa** (Easter Week) brings with it various spectacular processions day and night, especially in the more traditional working-class neighborhoods. The somber *penitentes,* shrouded in hoods and shouldering enormous images of the Virgin Mary and Christ on the Cross eerily recall the days of the Inquisition.

May: **Festimad** (tel 531–77–00; Círculo de Bellas Artes, Marqués de Casa Riera, 2; metro Banco de España) is a weeklong celebration of the alternative arts scene, including photography, sculpture, multimedia installations, poetry readings, dance performances, and concerts of every kind of music from acoustic jazz to a cappella to ambient. The **San Isidro Festival**, held May 8–15, honors Madrid's patron saint, a 12th-century laborer renowned for aiding the poor and sick (contact tourist office for more information; see below). Concerts, dances, and mini-festivals highlighting everything from china to rare books, are held throughout the city in bars, plazas, and arts venues. This celebration also ushers in a three-week period of bullfights featuring top matadors and prize bulls from around Spain. With all the groupies hanging about, they ought to rechristen the San Isidro festival the "Running of the Bullfighters."

June: **Festival Mozart** (tel 356–76–22, *Scherzo* magazine, for concerts and venues) is a two-month gala featuring the works of Mozart and his contemporaries.

July: **Veranos de la Villa** (tel 580–25–75, Comunidad de Madrid; or tel 588–16–36, Patronato Municipal de Turismo), a summer-long cultural extravaganza sponsored by the city, includes cinema retrospectives, opera, flamenco, theater, and pop performances by such artists as Paco de Lucia, B. B. King, and Elvis Costello.

September: **Festival de Otoño** (tel 580–25–75) is a highly regarded autumn arts festival. The various theater pieces, dance concerts, recitals, and exhibitions usually center around a theme (such as a specific country's cultural contributions or a literary figure like Salomé).

November: **Festival Internacional de Jazz** (tel 447–64–00, Colectivo Promoción Jazz) brings prominent performers like Wynton Marsalis and Tito Puente.

Gay and lesbian resources... The free *Shangay Express* is the most informative publication, featuring complete listings of bars and discos and up-to-the-minute dish on what's happening where. **Gai Inform** (tel 523–00–70; 5–9pm) is a live information line for residents and tourists alike, providing details on everything from meetings to tourist activities to health matters.

Mail... There are few district post offices, and their hours (9am–2pm) are hardly night-owl-friendly. The fastest and easiest way to purchase stamps is to stop by one of the many *estancos* (tobacconist's shops). Postcards and letters to the U.S. under 20 grams cost 114 ptas. and generally take a week to arrive. But whether you feel like writing postcards to Aunt Agnes or not, a trip to the main post office, the centrally-located **Palacio de Comunicaciones** (Plaza de Cibeles; open Mon–Fri 8am–10pm; Sat 8:30am–10pm) is a Madrid must. This multi-tiered edifice is best described as cuckoo rococo or "meshuGothic" (after the Yiddish word for "crazy"). Constructed between 1904 and 1918 at the height (or depth) of Art Nouveau extravagance, this deliciously garish monument is an appropriate enthronement of petty bureaucracy. The interior, with its cathedral ceilings and polished marble floors, is even more elaborate—you half expect Norma Desmond to glide down the ornate stairway, or the employees to break into a Busby Berkeley number. Cliffie from "Cheers" would be proud!

Money matters... The unit of currency is the *peseta* (pta.), which has undergone several devaluations in recent years as Spain's extraordinary economic boom began to recede. The smallest bill is 1,000 ptas.; coins come in denominations of 1, 5, 10, 25, 50, 100, 200, and 500 ptas. Most major hotels offer a decent exchange rate; in a pinch, you can always check out one of the *cambios* (exchange booths) along the main thoroughfare, Gran Vía. The fact that many stay open as late as 4am and waive their commission doesn't compensate for the usurious rates. Needless to say, there's a currency exchange service at the airport. Banks usually offer a better deal, but commissions and exchange rates vary significantly; always go to the major offices rather than the local branches. A passport is usually required, whether for credit card transactions, cash, or traveler's checks. Your biggest savings, if you're changing at least $100, is at ATM's, most of which accept American bank cards.

Newspapers and magazines... Madrid has three major newspapers: **ABC, El Mundo,** and **El País.** All three list all-night pharmacies and devote several pages to the arts (with daily film, gallery, concert, and theater listings). The latter two have substantial national and international sections, and on Friday both offer a separate arts and nightlife section; the glossy **Metrópoli** (*El Mundo*) is usually more adventurous in content than **Tentaciones** (*El País*), but the latter counters with intelligent arts coverage in its Saturday pull-out. As for their editorial slants, *El País* leans to the left and *El Mundo* (which delighted in exposing the scandals that helped bring down the Socialist Party in 1996) to the right, though neither is in imminent danger of teetering over.

The weekly **Guía del Ocio** is an invaluable roundup of every conceivable event held in the city, as well as an encyclopedic source for bars, clubs, restaurants, cinemas, and theaters. The related articles are uninspired and simplistic—even the español-challenged may be able to pick their way through.

The International Herald Tribune and numerous British papers are available at leading newsstands and bookstores. **In Madrid,** available in cafes and bookstores, is a free English monthly "for the hip, cool, and transient"; it offers some cogent commentary on the club scene but its listings are woefully inaccurate and out of date.

Opening and closing times... Shops are usually open from 9:30am to 2pm and 5 to 8:30pm Monday through Saturday. Banks are open 9am to 2pm Monday through Friday.

Public transportation... Madrid's subway system—the **Metro**—is efficient and comprehensive, and while the stations are sterile, they're safe, well-lit, and graffiti-less (though you'll find the usual complement of bazaars, beggars, and bogus musicians at major stops). There are 10 lines, and the *correspondencias* (transfer points) are clearly marked. The trains run between 6am and 1:30am. Tickets cost 130 ptas.; a ticket good for ten rides—ask for a *bono* or deposit the money in an automatic dispensing machine—is a bargain at 660 ptas. There are 170 bus lines, many of which are useful for trips to outlying areas of the city, but since the buses are often slowed by Madrid's heavy traffic and stop running around 11:30pm, the subway is often the better choice for getting around

MADRID ⟋ DOWN AND DIRTY

town. Bus tickets are 130 ptas.; a ten-trip **Bonobús** ticket (available only at *estancos* (tobacconist's shops), newsstands, and the EMT kiosks) costs 660 ptas. Insert the ticket into the machine to the left of the driver when you board; there are no free transfers.

Smoking... It seems that smoking is not only permitted but actively encouraged throughout Madrid (even in the airport and hospital waiting rooms!). There are no smoking-free sections in any public spaces, no smoking-free rooms in hotels, and given that it's considered impolite to ask someone not to smoke in a bar or restaurant, it's extremely doubtful anyone here has even considered doing a study on the effects of second-hand smoke.

Taxis... Cabs are relatively inexpensive and you can hail them easily from the street, even after the metro stops running at 1:30am. A green light and/or yellow neon *Libre* sign on the outside of the cab indicates that it's free. The meter starts at 175 ptas. and then ticks along at the rate of 5 ptas. for every 1/12th kilometer or 30 seconds of waiting time.

Telephones... Even Spaniards complain about the outrageous tolls charged for international calls by Telefónica, the national phone monopoly. Thank God for **AT&T** (access number: 900–990–011) and **MCI** (access number: 900–990–014) calling cards. If you must place a direct call, avoid using your hotel phone unless you're on a fat expense account. At phone centers called *locutorios* you're assigned a booth and you pay the amount in full when your call is terminated; the rates are still scandalous, but at least you're not paying double. The three most convenient centers are at Gran Vía, 30 (open until midnight); Paseo de Recoletos, 41 (open until midnight); and the Palacio de Comunicaciones (Plaza de Cibeles, open until 10pm). When calling to Madrid from other parts of Spain, first dial 91 (Madrid's area code). When calling from the States, first dial 34 (the country code for Spain), then 1 (the city code for Madrid).

Tickets... FNAC (tel 595–61–00; Calle Preciados, 28; open daily 10am–10pm), a discount book and music superstore, sells concert and theater tickets. **Madrid Rock** (tel 523–26–52; Gran Vía, 25; open daily 10:30am–3pm, 4:30–9:30pm), a record store, is the main outlet for tickets to rock and pop concerts.

Time... Written Spanish uses the 24-hour clock (known as "military time" in the U.S.); hence when a restaurant posts its dinner hours as "21:00–23:30," it means chowtime is from 9 to 11:30pm. No one, however, will order you to meet them at "22:00 hours." Spain is six hours ahead of Eastern Standard Time (the Canary Islands only five). As in the U.S., daylight savings time begins in mid-April and lasts until mid-October.

Tipping... Though service is included at most restaurants, it's still customary to leave a 5- to 10-percent tip. Except for leaving leftover small change, nobody tips at bars. Cabbies expect a nominal tip (5 percent is sufficient). Porters count on 100–200 ptas. per bag.

Tourist information... Both the city tourist office, **Patronato Municipal de Turismo** (tel 588–16–36; Plaza Mayor, 3 ; open Mon–Fri 10am–8pm, Sat 10am–2pm), and the regional tourist board, **Comunidad de Madrid** (tel 419–49–51; Duque de Medinaceli, 2; open Mon–Fri 9am–7pm, Sat 9am–1pm; also an information booth at the airport), can provide limited information, from city maps to brochures in English. The Patronato puts out two basic but free pamphlets, the weekly events guide *En Madrid* and the bi-monthly *Enjoy Madrid.* The newspapers and the weekly *Guía del Ocio* are far more helpful about specific events and locales.

Traveling for the disabled... Madrid is hardly in the vanguard when it comes to providing for the physically challenged. Ramps are still almost unheard of, few public toilets (let alone hotel bathrooms) have railings, and even fewer elevators have instructions in Braille. Even if they were properly equipped, most public facilities are so cramped there's little room for maneuverability for people built like matchsticks, let alone for those using wheelchairs or walking sticks. The major museums are the most enlightened institutions, providing elevators and ramps for their visitors. All buses have seats behind the driver that are nominally reserved for people who have difficulty walking, and there are a few wheelchair-accessible buses (roughly a quarter of the fleet). The metro is a disgrace: plenty of stairs and no elevators. Contact the **Coordinadora de Minusválidos Físicos de Madrid** aka **COMFE** (tel 413–74–41; María Guzmán, 52; metro Nuevos Ministerios; open Mon–Fri 8am–3pm) for the latest developments and general information.

BARCELONA BY NIGHT

what's
hot,
what's
not

Barcelona, 8am: the after-hours clubs are disgorging customers by the dozens. The all-night revelers stagger blinking into the light, colliding with the more sedate, bourgeois Catalans taking their morning constitutional. A dominatrix with her male slave on a leash passes a chic Chanel-clad matron being dragged by her Great Dane. Neither of these ladies pays any attention to the other; Barcelona's residents are notoriously tolerant of their fellow citizens' nocturnal habits.

No matter what their age, social status, or sexual orientation, all Barcelonans share an affinity for starting the night later than North Americans do. The course of nighttime pursuits follows the general pattern established in Madrid (see What's Hot, What's Not for Madrid).

Another constant—at any hour of the day or night—is Barcelona's breathtaking beauty. Almost any block offers stop-and-gape architecture, and many neighborhoods evoke other centuries. Just walking from one club to another, down a narrow medieval street crowded with wrought-iron balconies or by stone walls built by the Romans that gleam in the moonlight, may rank among your best memories of a night on the town.

What's hot

DJs rule... The international circuit supplies Barcelona's seemingly unquenchable appetite for spin masters. Often into heavy techno, the DJs at places like the **Apolo, La Boîte, Jimmy'z** or **KGB** add their own twists to the mix of music that keeps people on their feet until long after sunrise.

Water, water... When municipal authorities opened Barcelona to the sea at the turn of the decade by tearing down the dilapidated warehouses and rail yards that had blocked access to the waterfront and replacing them with an urban paradise of walkways and new construction, the city's nightlife took a definite turn toward the port. There are no neighbors there to complain about late-late partyers, and on a warm night the sea breeze is a particular pleasure. Scores of clubs, bars, and restaurants have sprung up along the harbor from the **Maremagnum** mall just across from the Ramblas, through **Barceloneta** all the way to the **Port Olímpica**.

Sex... Barcelona, more than any other place in Spain, has always had a reputation for sexual tolerance, even, to a limited degree, during the harsh years of the Franco dictatorship. Now the city is known as one of the most sexually open in western Europe, whether it be straight, gay, lesbian, bi, sadomasochistic, or fetishistic. Catalans apparently accept whatever goes on as long as it doesn't disrupt their own lives. **Bagdad** has a hard-core show that would make a sailor blush. At **La Amistad** you can swap mates with another couple, or keep yours and add a third. None of these places are in danger of being shut down by authorities. Nor are the numerous sex shops, like the **Sextienda** for gay men, or the **Blue Box** or **Magic America** for heterosexuals.

Personal security... Unfortunately, your valuables might become what's hot if you don't keep an eye and a grip on your purse, packages, camera, wallet, and the like in public places. Violent crime is low in Barcelona, but there's a lot of theft. Travelers should take a cue from the fact that the locals here take their radios out of their cars and into the bar or movie theater with them in the evening. Your stay here will be enhanced if you take a few precautions.

What's not

Designer bars... They were all the rage in the late seventies and into the mid-eighties, and some 50 of them opened within a decade. Many have sunk out of sight, but at clubs like **Network, Torres de Ávila**, and **Nick Havana** you can still get a look at what happens when you turn a contemporary designer loose to create a personal fantasy of what a bar should look like in a world ruled by chrome, television screens, and the hunt for 15 minutes of pop fame.

Java joints... All of a sudden, just after the 1992 Summer Olympics, coffee bars began popping up like the proverbial mushrooms after a rain. Everywhere you looked was a nicely decorated, dark-wood bar percolating with debate, where you could count on being able to get a cup of Blue Mountain from Jamaica, a cappuccino, or one of many other varieties of the blessed bean. Most of the places were just a little too snooty. Now they've either disappeared, or calmed down to the level of a neighborhood cafe.

Religion... Catalans are not nearly as Catholic as they once were, and the Church's control is no longer absolute; in many quarters, papal bull has taken on a new meaning. Today, Catalans are indifferent to how anyone feels about Jesus or whether or not one is a churchgoer. Birth control is so widely practiced that Catalans have the lowest birth rate in the world. And they see nothing wrong with women baring their breasts on the beach. As with their sexual practices, people's religious beliefs are considered to be their own business.

7

the club scene

A bevy of Scandinavian Valkyries in tank tops and Lycra shorts attack the dance floor with a dashiki-clad cadre of Senegalese exchange students. Two Brit sailors argue over an indifferent spiky-haired girl in combat fatigues, who leans against a column chain-smoking. Sweeping lasers briefly illuminate a half-undressed couple making out in a corner. Out of nowhere, the DJ switches from Marilyn Manson to a disco-fied Catalan folk song and the dancers spontaneously erupt in the joyful, enormously complex national dance called the *sardana*—not unlike "Hava Nagila" with a hip-swiveling Latin beat and even more stomps per second. Welcome to Barcelona, the United Nations of the young-and-restless club circuit, where the international crowd ranges from grand to grunge and cosmopolitan to cosmically way out.

Barcelona's club scene makes one yearn to be forever young. Its night crawlers typically just begin stretching their legs at 4am; they won't leave the dance floor until 8am—and that's on a weekday, when they have to head home, change clothes, shower, and get to work by 9. Weekends the *serious* partying is interrupted by meals and sleep—only when absolutely necessary.

Barcelona is a city for students and 20-somethings, though the merely young-at-heart also clog the city's main arteries in search of a good time. Unlike madrileños, who exercise copious amounts of stamina and dedication once night falls, when the citizens of Barcelona reach their mid-30s the equally intense Catalan work ethic kicks in like an activated dormant gene. This workaholic temperament seems to be reflected in the clubs' drab, prison-like interiors. Other than that, though, Barcelona's clublife certainly qualifies as the cutting-edge alternative-to the-alternative. The frolic ranges from all-night dancing to performance pieces, and in addition to the usual techno beat, Barcelona's clubs offer a smorgasbord of sounds. And the city is definitely on the World Music map; groups from Africa, South America, the States, and the Caribbean regularly appear in the jazz, rock, and salsa clubs, which also feature an ample reservoir of homegrown talent ranging from Spanish flamenco to Catalan rock.

Of course, there are clubs for the more mature as well, ranging from splendid 19th-century dance halls where you can practice your ballroom dancing to places where you can trade spouses with other couples and consummate your pleasure on the premises. Post-Franco decadence plays a role here just as it does in Madrid.

There's a porn palace where explicit sex is performed before your eyes, and, for those who prefer a more subtle approach, there are cabarets where the sex is more implicit and mixed with music, dance, and large amounts of clever ribaldry. As Hemingway wrote of another city, the Barcelona night is a moveable feast. Expect the unexpected, as a club shifts moods and clientele with the rapidity of a strobe light. Blink and you might miss something.

Getting Past the Velvet Rope

If you've mastered Madrid's doormen, you'll do fine in Barcelona. The opening and closing times are the same as Madrid, and most of Barcelona's clubs charge a cover, usually around 1,000 ptas., but it almost always pays for your first drink as well.

THE CLUB SCENE ☾ INTRODUCTION

Clubs in Central Barcelona

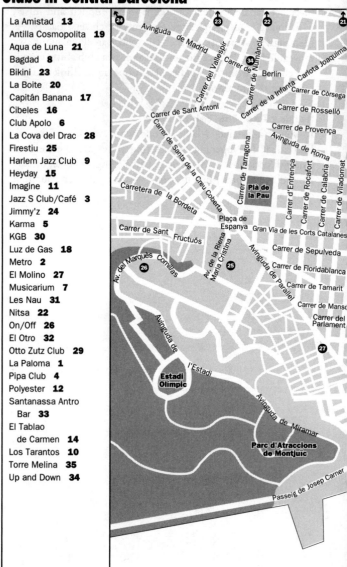

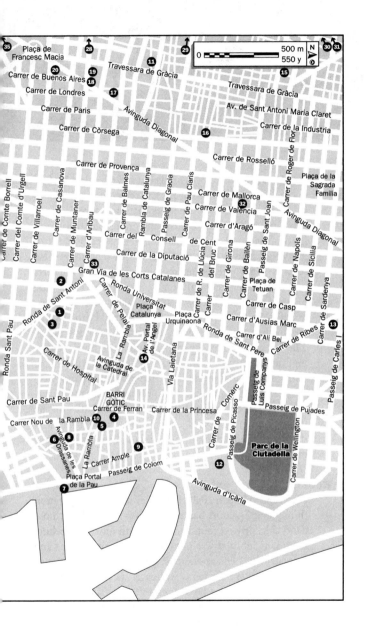

The Lowdown

Moveable clubs... It switches venues like Imelda Marcos once changed shoes, but **La Colectiva del Caracol** is worth trying to find for parties that are a jumble of art exhibits, slide projections, and nonstop throbbing music. The local *Okupa* movement—basically clubs of partying squatters that take over empty buildings—also spawns some interesting cultural events and concerts not commercial enough for clubs paying rent. One mainstay is **Les Nau**, which has taken over an abandoned textile factory in the Gràcia neighborhood. It's an old shoe factory converted to art and dance studios. The latter is an ideal spot for listening to music, dancing, or just sitting around and watching it all roll by; both provide a spontaneous, free-wheeling party with the under-30 avant-garde. Combined with the provisional feel, the work on the walls and the outfits on the floor are often just wild enough to make you feel that the thought police might burst in and break it up at any moment.

Rockin' Catalan cats... Groups like Sopa de Cabra, Els Pets, and Umpah Pah have developed a reputation throughout Spain. A band to watch is Peanut Pie, whose danceable, driving sound is tinged with funk and techno. **Bikini**, a club that was popular in the early eighties and reopened in 1995, is the best place to to hear up-and-coming local performers. Although its original patrons may now no longer be staying out until sunrise, a new generation has taken over this big, elegant club, which has a cocktail lounge, a room for disco and live music, and beyond these, a *salsoteca*. All three rooms are jammed and jamming at 2am with the broadest cross-section in Barcelona, from industrial-booted teeny-boppers to 40ish divorcees teetering in high heels. At **Club Apolo**, you can hear live Catalan rock as well as live salsa and recorded house, tech, and indie amidst the decaying splendor of an old ballroom on the second floor of an amusement arcade. The rigorously up-to-date sound system and unwrinkled crowd help dispel the sense of better days gone by.

Dance 'til you drop... Depending on the DJ, the atmosphere at the **Otto Zutz Club** can be feverish. Although it's a nondescript space in an equally nondescript neighborhood, the people who hang out here are anything but nondescript. The club's three floors, with a bar on each, attract everyone from the buttoned-down to the liberally pierced. **Jimmy'z** offers one room where the dance music is strictly salsa and another where the sound is totally techno; both spaces are enormous yet sardine-packed with wannabe beautiful people. **El Otro's** dance floor is small, the relaxed crowd shoulder-to-shouldering and smoldering on the floor and at the long bar. The populace is avant-garde but unguarded, with minimal posturing and posing, and the excellent sound system brings you everyone from Dylan to Zap Mama. Expect to stand a lot, because other than a couple of dozen stools, there's no place to sit. **Karma** is nirvana for a young and lively crowd, mostly students, who boogie to sounds spun by a techno-oriented DJ. This gamey basement room is so packed on weekends you have to escape outside periodically to breathe. You won't find many students at **Up and Down** unless they're getting their MBAs. The club has two levels—upstairs features expensive food, while downstairs the young, wealthy, and hip dance the night away. **Club Apolo** offers a late-night (until 6am) techno bash on Thursdays and trip-hop/jungle music on Fridays. The striking **La Luna Mora** was an instant hit with the monied young set as much for its strong design (curving walls and a glass floor upstairs) as for the quality of its sound system, which pumps Top-40 pop. If you're over 25 you should get a senior citizen's discount at **Satanassa Antro Bar**, where you might get turned away if you look like you're too old to still be living with your parents. This is a popular spot for young gay men, but the crowd is definitely mixed. The music is techno, and the nod to Satan in the name sets the tone.

The latest of the late... To finish up a long night out, try the ultra-trendy **Polyester** next to the Estació de França, where gay and straight alike get it on to the recorded techno. **KGB**, a soulless warehouse space in the residential Gràcia neighborhood, is another good spot to find that late-night techno-blast. At this cold war fantasy of grim straight lines and sharp corners, the clientele is varied and the dress code surprisingly loose—anything from torn T-shirts to prep blazers and rep ties. At shadowy, subterranean **Nitsa**, there's a roomy revolving dance floor and an insistent head-banging beat; it's a frequent stop on the international DJ route. If you need a break—and you very well might—you can go upstairs to the less hard-core *salsoteca*. Wealthy 20-somethings congregate at **On/Off** in the Poble Espanyol around 6am; on Saturday and Sunday mornings at 9 they're still dancing against the backdrop of twin screens showing psychedelic slide projections.

Flamenco: Spain's soul music... Catalonians have never been as impassioned about flamenco as other Spaniards—but Barcelona is increasingly attracting touring artists and developing its own talents. **Los Tarantos** used to be just for tourists, but since the Mas brothers (who also own the jazz club La Boite) took over, it has become venue of choice for both performers and local enthusiasts. The show's the thing here, with about sixty wooden folding seats, minimally decorated stage, low ceiling, and brick walls, on one of which is an attractive combination mosaic/painting of a dancer. The sound is good, and the singers, guitarists, and dancers are literally in your face. The studiedly authentic **El Tablao de Carmen** presents flamenco shows in the Poble Espanyol, the re-created Spanish village with exhibits on life in different parts of Spain, but along with the expected tourists there are plenty of locals; the show, while expensive, will not disappoint.

Not as cool as they claim... If your idea of a disco is international businesspeople loosening their ties and shedding their inhibitions, check out **Jimmy'z**, located in the basement of a four-star hotel. The almost-youngish crowd here is cheek-by-jowl, cheek-by-cheek, and very cheeky—a grabby grab bag of singles. They flaunt their couturier fashions as if they vanna be Ivana and flash their money as if they were trying to trump the Donald. **On/Off** is set in the hokey Poble Espanyol, a re-creation of several traditional villages around Spain (think Plymouth, Massachusetts meets Colonial Williamsburg). But the uptown kiddies who make the pilgrimage to get down here are anything but puritanical. The name also suits, since the style factor oscillates wildly from night to night. **Up and Down** features a similar see-and-be-scene and more door 'tude than necessary given the undistinguished surroundings. Any place jocks hang out may be automatically suspect as truly hip, and this is where the stars from the city's world-class soccer team, El Barça, like to hang out and act boorish.

All that jazz.... The esteemed **Harlem Jazz Club**, deep in the heart of the *barri gotic*, holds only about six tables, but that contributes to the joint's warm and friendly feeling. Small as the Harlem Jazz Club is, it's not as tiny as the **Pipa Club**, where the jazz club is squeezed inside a pipe collectors' club. The Pipa Club hosts sets by top local players in everything from straight-ahead jazz to Brazilian rhythms, and the sound system is more than adequate for the minute room. Classy **La Cova del Drac**, usually packed, books the best in local jazz, such as the internationally renowned Catalan pianist Tete Montoliu; also catches younger groups like the International Jazz Quartet on their world tours. The crowd is knowledgeable, though more sedate than in most old-town locations. Those in a less formal mood can contribute to the semi-anarchy of the **Jazz Sí Club/Café**, near the Sant Antoni market. Run by Barcelona's contemporary music school, Tallers de Music, it's where up-and-coming students get a chance to perfect their chops in public. Thursday evening jam sessions here begin at the unheard-of early hour of 8:30pm, and the place closes by 11. The modest entrance to **La Boîte** is a surprisingly comfortable basement room where the music ranges from avant-garde to Chicago blues, and the middle-class, uptown crowd is attentive and appreciative.

Cabaret the night away... **El Molino** (The Windmill) is a Barcelona institution: it's to Barcelona's Avenida Parallel what the Moulin Rouge is to Montmartre in Paris. El Molino is one broad wink, an old-fashioned, lecherous, macho leer at the world, its comics relentless in their pursuit of no-level-too-low. The dancers, though, have impeccable timing. Even the groups of older women on a wives' night out seem to enjoy it. At **La Luz de Gas**, where you can sit close to the stage without having to be on top of it. A weekend jazz venue, it offers a cabaret revue during the week that continues on in the spirit of the inimitable Dolly Van Doll, a transsexual whose two-hour cabaret revue was a staple of Barcelona nightlife for 20 years.

Dance hall nights... **La Paloma**, operating since 1902, is a huge, gilded place with rococo decor, down to the plush red velvet banquettes. Earlier on, an older crowd two-steps and waltzes to a live band. The club is a testament to the revivifying power of touch-dancing: even infirm aged couples seem magically to lose their limps while gliding around the floor. As the night wears on, the crowd grows younger, and music more up-tempo—hotter cha-chas, more soulful boleros. But even at 2am, you're likely to spot 60-ish señoritas launching into an impromptu cancan that exposes more flesh than would be decent at an earlier hour. A more subdued alternative is **Cibeles**, built in 1940 without the decorative excess of La Paloma. The excellent house orchestra has been playing here so long that they can perfectly gauge what the crowd of the moment is in to from fox-trot to salsa.

Tropical rhythms... **Antilla Cosmopolita** draws a wide range of listeners and dancers for live salsa Sunday through Thursday from some world-class performers; on weekends it becomes a *salsoteca*, with the latest sounds from the Caribbean blasting and slinky men and women practically glued to one another on the decent-sized dance floor. **Agua de Luna** offers free salsa classes on Wednesday and Thursday nights, and tango classes on Sunday nights. Despite its clichéd exotic touches (a thatch-covered bar dominates one corner), it's a big favorite for its wide wooden dance floor, dynamic live performers, and a sinuous, incredibly danceable recorded Latin mix. There are also occasional salsa concerts at that relatively old chestnut of a nightclub, **Bikini**, which attracts a more mature bunch; most of the aging girls from Ipanema should trade in their thongs for one-piece numbers on the beach. If you just want to listen, the lovely and comfortable cabaret **La Luz de Gas** devotes weekends to some of the city's best live Cuban and Latin jazz. It's a little gem of a theater/cabaret where you can hear boleros or salsa up close and personal.

For the gay of heart... Capitán Banana is a very hot disco catering to transvestites, drag queens, and the leather crowd (which has been known to unleash a few whips-and-chains fantasies on the dance floor). More discreet from midnight to 2am, the action gets decidedly wilder as the night wears on. The more down to earth **Heyday** draws a mixed crowd of lesbians, gay men, and a smattering of straight people. This comfortable, dimly lit disco with plenty of room to dance is no steamy pick-up joint; come here with a friend just for the fun of it to wind down after 4am. Gay men of all ages and proclivities crowd **Metro** on weekends for the superb house/techno mix and for private socializing in the back rooms. There's lighter pop music on the sound system at **Imagine**, which is popular with lesbians—a mix of locals and foreigners—and some companionable gay men. **Satanassa Antro Bar** is nicknamed "Satan's place" by locals. The decor is certainly irreverent and even borders on the blasphemous: the front room is plastered with candy hearts (which dozens of people lick over the course of the evening) and Catholic church memorabilia (stained glass, votive candles, wooden saints, and crucifixes) to which obese drag queens make obeisance. This is one of those gay hangouts that's become a must stop on the straight tourists' night crawl.

Pure sex... If a $50 admission charge doesn't put you off—though you do get one drink with that!—head for **Bagdad**. You can have dinner too, or just watch couples and trios getting it on onstage, and maybe even getting rubbed up against as they descend to the dance floor between sex acts. This place makes table-dancing seem as tame as burlesque. But club sex isn't necessarily a spectator sport; several clubs allow you to put the trois in menage or swap mates. In theory, no professionals work these locales, which tend to be short-lived. **La Amistad** is the most established. It offers pop and salsa in the front room, a second room and second dance floor for "slow dances," and a third area with lockers, showers, and cubicles with beds.

THE CLUB SCENE ⟍ THE LOWDOWN

Under the big top... That's right: tents. For serious danc-ing and heavy partying during the summer, visit one of the *carpas* put up every year between June 1 and August 31 just for those purposes. **Firestiu** is a group of 16 white tents that shelter 16 different bars, all of which share a large central dance space. If staying in the tents to dance begins to pall, you can switch to other diversions like bungee-jumping and mini-golf. Another group of white tents, down by the port, is **Musicarium**, which tends to attract the over-30 crowd. It's worth coming here just for the nighttime view of the port. Meanwhile, **Torre Melina** includes the temporary summer versions of a higher class of club under its seasonal big top—places like **Jimmy'z**. Numerous other tent sites spring up every summer, espe-cially on the waterfront by the Maremagnum and the Port Olimpic, and there's an 18-tent venue on Montjuïc.

The Club Scene: Index

Agua de Luna. Whether live music or recorded is featured, salsa devotees are dancing here. *Tel 410–04–40. Viladomat, 211; buses 43, 44. Open Tue–Thur 8pm–4am, Fri–Sat 10pm–5am.* **(see p. 142)**

La Amistad. It bills itself as a *Pub Liberal,* and, indeed, almost anything goes, from dress to behavior.... *Tel 231–04–53. Ausiàs Marc, 145; Marina metro stop. Open Mon–Sun 10pm–3am.* **(see p. 143)**

Antilla Cosmopolita. Draws a big dance crowd on the weekends with its strong salsa programming.... *Tel 200–77–14. Muntaner, 244; buses 6, 33, 58, 64, N8. Open Fri–Sat 11pm–6am.* **(see p. 142)**

Bagdad. Live sex shows, dinner, and dancing.... *Tel 442–07–77. 105 Nou Carrer de la Rambla, 105; Parallel metro stop. Continuous shows Mon–Sat 11pm–3am.* **(see p. 143)**

Bikini. Catalan rock, salsa, house—you never know what's going to turn up here, but it's bound to be good. Located underground in the l'Illa shopping mall.... *Tel 322–00–05. Deu i Mata, 105; Les Corts metro stop; buses 15, 43, 59. Open Mon–Thur 7pm–4:30am; weekends until 6am.* **(see pp. 138, 142)**

La Boîte. Small and usually packed jazz venue.... *Tel 419–59–50. Avda. Diagonal, 477; buses 7, 15, 33, 63, 68. Open Sun–Thur 11pm–5:30am; weekends 11pm–6am.* **(see p. 141)**

Capitán Banana. Drag disco par excellence.... *Tel 202–14–30. Moià, 1; bus N8. Open Sun–Thur 12:30pm–5am, weekends until 6am.* **(see p. 143)**

Cibeles. Two floors of old-fashioned, grand ballroom/dance-hall ambience.... *Tel 457–38–77. Córsega, 36; Diagonal metro stop. Open Thur, Fri 11:30pm–5am; Sat 6pm–5am; Sun 6–9:30pm.* **(see p. 142)**

Club Apolo. Thursday and Friday are for techno or trip-hop; Saturday and Sunday for salsa and the occasional live performance of Catalan rock.... *Tel 441–40–01. Nou de la Rambla, 113; Parallel metro stop. Open Thur–Fri midnight–6am; Sat–Sun 10pm–6am.* **(see p. 139)**

La Colectiva del Caracol. This *very* alternative collective moves from space to space. Call Wagner (tel 451–76–45) to find out about upcoming events, or inquire at one of their favorite clubs, El Otro (see below). **(see p. 138)**

La Cova del Drac. An uptown jazz club with consistently high-quality performers—local bands during the week, occasional internationally known touring groups on weekends.... *Tel 200–70–32. Vallmajor, 33; buses 14, 58, 64, N8. Open Mon–Thur 10pm–4am; Fri–Sat 9pm–4am, closed Aug.* **(see p. 141)**

Firestiu. Summertime entertainment set out under tents.... *Tel 322–03–26. Plaça del Univers; Espanya metro stop. Open June–Sept, Thur–Sat 10pm–5am.* **(see p. 144)**

Harlem Jazz Club. Tiny, it's still one of the city's oldest and best jazz clubs. Live music around 9–10pm.... *Tel 310–07–55. Comtessa de Sobrediel, 8; Jaume I metro stop. Open Tue–Sun 10:30am–4am; Closed Aug. No cover charge.* **(see p. 141)**

Heyday. A relaxed place for couples of the same sex, whichever it may be. You'll get a ticket on your way in, have it punched for every drink, and pay the total on the way out.... *Bruiniquer, 59–61; Joanic metro stop. Open daily 10:30pm–5am. One drink minimum.* **(see p. 143)**

Imagine. (Mostly) lesbian disco.... *María Cubí, 4; buses 16, 17, 27. Open Fri, Sat 11pm–3am; Sun 7pm–midnight.* **(see p. 143)**

Jazz Sí Club/Café. A cramped, lively venue for live jazz by students.... *Tel 329–00–20. Requessens, 2; Sant Antoni metro stop. Open 9am–11pm.* **(see p. 141)**

Jimmy'z. This hotel nightclub features DJs, dancing, and a singles scene.... *Tel 414–63–62. Hotel Princesa Sofía, Plaça Pius XII; María Cristina metro stop. Open Mon–Wed 11pm–4am, Thur–Sat 11pm–5am.* **(see pp. 139, 140, 144)**

Karma. Tunnel-like dance club in a cellar attracts lots of students.... *Tel 302–56–80. Plaça Reial, 10; Liceu metro stop. Bar open Tue–Sun 8:30pm–2:30am; disco Tue–Sun 11:30pm–4:30am.* **(see p. 139)**

KGB. Headbanger disco where things don't get started until after 3am.... *Tel 210–59–06. Alegre de Dalt, 55; Alfons X metro stop. Open 8am–5am daily.* **(see p. 140)**

Les Nau. An *Okupa* cultural center for music, art, dance, and theater as well as the occasional party.... *Alegre de Dalt, 52; Joanic metro stop.* **(see p. 138)**

La Luna Mora. Live music begins at midnight in this sleek new club down by the beach and the Hotel Arts.... *Tel 322–03–26. Marina Village Complex; Ciutadella/Vila Olímpica metro stop. Open Mon–Thur 10pm–4am, Fri–Sat 10pm–5am.* **(see p. 139)**

La Luz de Gas. Saturday nights are particularly hot, with Cuban and/or salsa rhythms; there's cabaret during the week.... *Tel 209–77—11. Muntaner, 246; buses 7, 15, 33, 58, 64. Open 11pm–5am daily.* **(see p. 142)**

Metro. For the single man looking for same.... *Tel 323–52–27. Sepúlveda, 185; Universitat metro stop; buses N4, N7. Open daily midnight–5am.* **(see p. 143)**

El Molino. A cabaret classic out of another era, all in good fun.... *Tel 441–63–83. Vila i Vila, 99; Parallel metro stop. Performances Tue–Fri at 6 and 11pm; Sat at 6pm, 10:30pm, 1am; Sun at 6pm.* **(see p. 141)**

Musicarium. Summer boogeying in tents, down by the

port.... *Tel 322–03–26. Port Vell, behind the Customs building; Drassanes metro stop. Open summer, Thur–Sat 10pm–5am.* **(see p. 144)**

Nitsa. If it's techno you want, welcome home.... *Tel 458–62–50. Plaça Joan Llongueres, 1–3; buses 6, 7, 33, 34, 63, 68. Open Thur–Sat midnight–6am.* **(see p. 140)**

On/Off. Disco at the Poble Espanyol, open very late and popular with rich kids.... *Tel 423–96–40. Cani de la Fuxarda, behind Poble Espanyol; Espanya metro stop. Open Fri, Sat 4am–8:30am all year, Wed–Sun 5:30–8:30am in Julu and Aug.* **(see pp. 140, 141)**

El Otro. Crowded, friendly, and popular with avant-garde youth.... *Tel 323—67—59. Valencia, 166; Hospital metro stop. Admission charge. Open 10:30am–3am daily; closed Aug.* **(see p. 139)**

Otto Zutz Club. Big and bland, but a good place to talk, dance, or watch the dancing.... *Tel 238–07–22. Lincoln, 15; buses 16, 17, 25 27, 127. Open Tue–Sat 11pm–6am.*
(see p. 139)

La Paloma. It's a ballroom out of another era. Check out the view from the balcony.... *Tel 301–68–97. Tigre, 27; Universitat metro stop. Open Thur–Sat 6–5am, Sun 6–9:30pm.*
(see p. 142)

Pipa Club. Upstairs club with displays of pipes from around the world and a comfortable bar; live jazz shows Thursday–Saturday.... *Tel 302–47–32. Plaça Reial, 3; Liceu metro stop. Open 10pm–5am daily.* **(see p. 141)**

Polyester. The most popular of late-late-night places to dance.... *No phone. Estació de França; Avda. Marqués de Argentera; Barceloneta metro stop. Open Fri, Sat from 1:30am until past dawn.* **(see p. 140)**

Satanassa Antro Bar. A favorite among a young, sexually ambiguous, pierced, hard-partying crowd.... *Tel 451–00–52. Aribau, 27; Universitat metro stop. Open 10:30pm–3:30am daily* **(see pp. 139, 143)**

El Tablao de Carmen. Tablao flamenco in the Poble Espanyol. If you make a reservation, you don't have to pay the Poble admission fee.... *Tel 325–68–95. Arcs, 9; buses 13, 61. Shows Tue–Sun 9:30 and 11pm. Cover charge includes drink.* **(see p. 140)**

Los Tarantos. Good flamenco at this tablao in the beautiful Plaça Reial.... *Tel 318–30–67. 17 Plaça Reial, 17; Liceu metro stop. Shows Mon–Sat 10:15–midnight. Cover charge includes 2 drinks.* **(see p. 140)**

Torre Melina. Uptown vibes, but essentially everyone's equal when they're shaking a leg under the tent.... *Tel 414–63–62. De la Torre Melina, off Avda. Diagonal; Universitat metro stop. Open June–Sept, Thur–Sat 9:30pm–5am.* **(see p. 144)**

Up and Down. Its popularity may be on the wane, but you can still watch the beautiful people here.... *Tel 280–29–22. Numancia, 179; María Cristina metro stop. Restaurant and upstairs dance floor open until 3am, downstairs until 5am; closed Sun, Mon.* **(see pp. 139, 141)**

8

the bar scene

A European Union study done a couple of years ago concluded that Spain has as many bars as the other 11 countries of the EU combined. As the country's second-largest city, Barcelona shoulders its fair share of that load. In fact, virtually every block of this international playground has at least one, and often more bars. Whatever part of town you stumble into, you're never far from a place to have a drink (with no cover charge). Even the humblest cafe has a full bar going no matter what the hour (hard-core partyers take their coffee with a hefty splash of cognac, a high-octane brew called a *carajillo*). And the variety of places runs the gamut from bustling yuppie fern bars (where locals often negotiate business, as well as romantic encounters) to quiet, dimly lit boîtes where you can count on the drinks being mixed just so and you can talk in the charged undertones of love without being overheard by the people at the next table.

Governed by a stricter protocol than the madrileños, Barcelonans rarely invite each other into their homes—they're much more likely to get together in a bar to socialize. Here, as in Madrid, drinking is more a convivial exercise than an attempt at oblivion (see introduction to Madrid Bar Scene for more information). Company cafeterias serve wine and beer and bosses don't bat an eye if employees have a frosty one on their morning coffee break. Similarly, at a bar you'll find some patrons having coffee, others drinking beer or cocktails. But while almost everyone drinks, and many do so long before what North Americans would think of as an acceptable hour, there are surprisingly few drunks. Sure, some youngster will occasionally get pretty rowdy after 2am, but most people are raised to regard alcohol as something to be used frequently but in moderation. Still, people *are* beginning to realize that the death and destruction caused by traffic accidents is often directly traceable to that last drink too many, and traffic stops and Breathalyzer tests are becoming more frequent, particularly on weekend nights. Be forewarned if you're driving.

There are still a number of so-called *bares americanos* (American bars) operating throughout the city, odd remnants of the later years of Franco's dictatorship. Far more prevalent here than in Madrid—perhaps reflecting Barcelona's port status (sailors, sailors, sailors!) and hedonistic reputation—these dives have a few heavily made-up women who work the customers (the lower the cleavage, the higher the price of drinks). You know the type of place, with garish neon cocktail signs and posters announcing "Chicas!" So remember, this ain't your friendly neighborhood joint that stocks your favorite scotch: you're more likely to see johns than Johnny Walker. Unless you're curious, avoid them: Barcelona has plenty of places where you can *ligar* (literally, connect) for free.

Bars are an important part of Barcelona's lifeblood, integral to its circulation system. Barcelona's residents never seem so relaxed, so at home in their city as when they're sitting outside a cafe in the warm evening air, kissing or talking. People are as at ease in their regular bars as in their living rooms. Finding one's own is half the fun. *Salut!*

The Beaten Path

The hottest new places to go for *copas* (drinks) are on the waterfront. Barcelona opened itself to the sea for the 1992 Summer Olympics, demolishing a long row of shabby warehouses that blocked access to the water and building walkways, restaurants, and the harborside mall, **Maremagnum**. You can drink (and in most places dance) all the way from Maremagnum to the string of small bars in the **Port Olímpic**, a few blocks north of **Barceloneta**, and then double back to the strip of bars along the palm-tree-lined **Moll de la Fusta**, which usually begin to fill late at night. Inland from the Moll de la Fusta and ever-popular with bar-hoppers is **La Ciutat Vella** (the Old City), which includes the neighborhoods of **La Ribera** and the **Barri Gòtic**, whose streets and barrooms will take you (even before you've started drinking) on a journey back through time, from the 19th century to the Middle Ages. While in the area, ramble the **Ramblas** for its turn-of-the-century cafes and bars and make your way to **El Raval**, a neighborhood built in the 1700s, many of whose streets do not appear to have changed much since. Part of this area has been called *el Barri Chino* since the turn of the century, although few if any Chinese have ever lived here (it's not advisable to wander here alone late at night). There's no need to spend all your drinking time in the Old City, however. Students congregate a little ways uptown, in **l'Eixample**, where designer bars flourish and tapas bars draw large crowds. Once you reach the **Avenida Diagonal**, you can start drinking your way out to increasingly classier barris.

What to Order

Whatever you please. If you want a draft beer, ask for a *caña*. A small bottle of beer is called a *quinto*; a *mediana* is larger. The local brewery is Damm. Their Estrella is a decent lager, Voll-Damm a richer brew, and Bock-Damm a passable dark beer. At most bars you'll find both scotch and bourbon, but if you ask for a "whiskey" you'll inevitably be served scotch. The best Catalan cognac is Mascaró, and now's your chance to try Havana Club, Cuba's best rum, which is not available in the States. For oenophiles, both the reds and whites from the Penedès region of Catalunya are well worth tasting. Be sure to try *cava*, Catalunya's version of champagne; the best are as crisp and dry as the desert (see Late Night Dining for Madrid for recommendations).

Etiquette

Most times, simple finger-pointing gets your desire across to the bartender. There's no need to tip, but most patrons leave their lose change if they feel they've been well-treated. Sixteen is the legal drinking age, but it's not enforced. Generally, anyone who can behave themselves while drinking is welcome to do so.

154

Bars in Central Barcelona

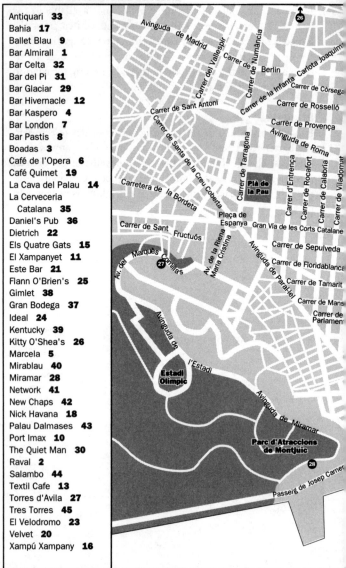

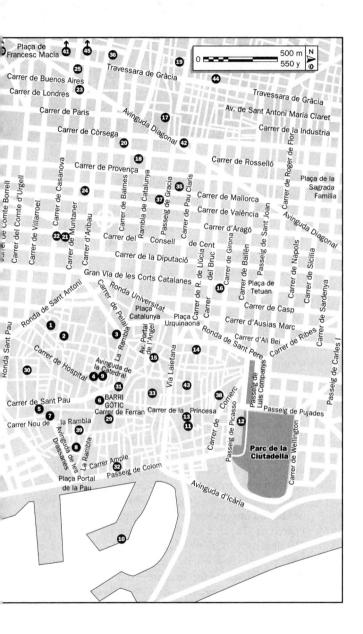

Plaça de Francesc Macià

Travessara de Gràcia

Carrer de Buenos Aires

Carrer de Londres

Carrer de Paris

Avinguda Diagonal

Carrer de Còrsega

Travessara de Gràcia

Av. de Sant Antoni Maria Claret

Carrer de la Industria

Carrer de Rosselló

Plaça de la Sagrada Familia

Carrer de Provença

Carrer de Mallorca

Carrer de València

Carrer d'Aragó

Avinguda Diagonal

Carrer de la Diputació

Carrer de Casanova

Carrer del Comte Borrell

Carrer del Comte d'Urgell

Carrer de Villaroel

Carrer de Muntaner

Carrer d'Aribau

Carrer de Balmes

Rambla de Catalunya

Passeig de Gràcia

Carrer de Pau Claris

Carrer de R. de Llúcia

del Bruc

Carrer de Girona

Carrer de Bailèn

Passeig de Sant Joan

Carrer de Napols

Carrer de Sicilia

Carrer de Roger de Flor

Carrer de Sardenya

Passeig de Carles I

Carrer del Consell de Cent

Gran Vía de les Corts Catalanes

Ronda Universitat

Plaça Catalunya

Plaça de Tetuan

Carrer de Casp

Carrer d'Ausias Marc

Carrer d'Ali Bei

Carrer de Ribes

Ronda de Sant Pere

Ronda de Sant Antoni

Carrer de Pelai

Ronda de Sant Pau

Carrer de Hospital

Plaça Urquinaona

Av. Portal de l'Angel

Avinguda de la Catedral

Vía Laietana

BARRI GÒTIC

Carrer de Sant Pau

Carrer de Ferran

Carrer de la Princesa

Carrer Nou de la Rambla

Avinguda de les Drassanes

La Rambla

Carrer Ample

Passeig de Colom

Passeig de Picasso

Passeig de Comerç

Passeig de Luis Companys

Passeig de Pujades

Parc de la Ciutadella

Carrer de Wellington

Plaça Portal de la Pau

Avinguda d'Icària

0   500 m
      550 y
N

Picasso drank here... Picasso had a special fondness for Barcelona (he lived here as a young man, from 1895 to 1904). We know he drank in **Els Quatre Gats**, a hangout for struggling artists when he himself was an unknown. These days it's tonier and more expensive, thanks to the hype. Go anyway to see the Picasso drawings, works by his friend and fellow painter, Ramón Casas (a cofounder of the bar), and the building (designed by Josep Puig i Cadafalch, probably the greatest of Barcelona's turn-of-the-century architects and a Gaudí protegé). Nab one of the marble-topped, two-person tables in the balcony for a cozy view of the scene. The narrow interior of **Bar del Pi**, another one-time Picasso hangout, is generally packed, but no matter; the best seats are outside in the plaça along the wall of the 15th-century Cathedral Del Pi—ringside for a diverse human parade of street musicians, fire-eaters, passers-by, gawking tourists, local ne'er-do-wells, and oddly furtive figures clearly up to no good.

Slumming It... Bar Glaciar is in the knock-down beautiful, if slightly sinister and seedy Plaça Reial (which sees its share of knock-down, drag-out *fights* among sailors, skin-heads, and prostitutes—it's living theater of the absurd). Glaciar is the kind of place you expect to find in a Hemingway or Graham Greene novel, with down-at-heels expatriates drowning their sorrows in cheap whisky. Anything's likely to happen here—and will. **Kentucky** is that rare *bar americano* with a true down-home feel. Named for a U.S. destroyer, it maintains its sailors-on-leave ambience thanks to yellowing photos of battleships and a classic sixties jukebox. Intellectual types love it (it's a favorite place to enjoy Americana kitsch while trashing it). Surprisingly, the atmosphere of incipient roughhousing lingers like the stale cigarette smoke. **Bar Pastis** is a little bit of Marseilles at the edge of the *Barri Chino*. And we mean little—a couple of tiny tables and some standing room, but there *is* lots of pastis (and not much else) behind the diminutive bar, and they've managed to plaster 50 years of clippings about the place on the walls. It's on a narrow little street just off the bottom of the Ramblas; you'll know you're in the right place when you see the transvestite prostitutes congregated at the door. Inside, you're likely to hear Edith Piaf, Charles Aznavour, Georges Moustaki, and Yves Montand on the defiantly Francophile, anachronistic sound system.

Historic haunts... Dating from the 1860s, **Bar Almirall** is the city's oldest continuously open bar; its turn-of-the-century Art Nouveau decor, peeling travel posters, and period furniture are studiedly down-at-heels, contrasting appealingly with the upscale, mostly youthful crowd. But be forewarned: you'll pay extra for imbibing in a landmark. **Textil Café** epitomizes old-world charm. Located on the patio of the medieval Palau dels Marquesos de Lliò (which currently houses the Textile Museum), it can carry you back six centuries, especially on a warm moonlit evening. It's run by gay men with a welcoming attitude toward straight, gay, and lesbian alike. **Bar London** has been popular ever since its opening in 1910. The cavernous room features mirrored walls, sensuous modernist fixtures—and a trapeze (not in use that we've ever seen) over the bar. The gregarious atmosphere is conducive to meeting the young Barcelonans and English-speaking travelers who flock here. The Barri Gòtic's **Antiquari** is aptly-named—there's a sense of age and solidity in its comfortable furniture, solid mahogany bar, antique wall tiles, and the bits of an ancient Roman wall still visible in the basement room. A seat at any of the trio of tables outside faces the stones of Plaça del Rei, where Columbus is said to have reported to Ferdinand and Isabella on his return from the New World. Another modernista bar is the **Café de l'Opera**, which has commanded the Ramblas since the 1920s. Its terraza, strategically positioned for maximum people-watching, is always crowded, popular among locals and foreigners alike. Barcelona's last truly grand turn-of-the-century cafe, its Gaudíesque but not gaudy decor alone makes it worth a stop.

Drinks with a view... From **Miramar** on top of Montjuïc (site of a medieval Jewish cemetery) you can look north across the sparkling lights of Barcelona to the sea. A lovely place to propose or let someone down easily. **Mirablau**, perched atop Tibidabo, offers recorded jazz, a comfortable room, and a view of the entire city stretched out and lit up below like a gaudy society matron wearing every carat she possesses. **Port IMAX**, overlooking the sea, is a swoony place to sit and hold hands, have an intimate conversation, or just watch the boats, as brightly colored as a child's finger painting, glide by. The music is kept unobtrusively low and the view soothing, which is why lovers, solitary postcard writers, and tired shoppers find their way here. Unfortunately, it's located at the IMAX cinema, and though you won't need a movie ticket to get to the bar, it can get crowded and touristy when a film has just let out.

Neighborhood joints... The clean lines, high ceilings, and (for Barcelona) unusual roominess of Gràcia's **Salambo**—plus the fact that their sandwiches are actually edible—all almost qualify it as a fern bar (the svelte clientele can often be seen munching on designer salads). But the two upstairs pool tables and almost zero pretension bring it down a few notches. If you're in the mood for some picking and strumming while you're in Gràcia, cramped and crumbling **Casa Quimet** has 200 guitars lining the walls, all of which are kept in tune for any patron who wants to play one. The owner's surly son recently took over, but no matter—it's worth having a look at all those guitars. **Raval** is a handsome two-floor bar, a big room where the music never gets louder than the conversation level, so the intellectual and artistic crowd that gathers here in the evening can pursue earnest discussions about everything from Bosch to Bosnia. **Bar Kasparo**, tucked away on a tranquil little Raval Plaça with a children's playground and lovely arcade, has a devoted following of young Barcelonans who actually enjoy having a conversation along with their drink or coffee. **El Velòdrom**, at the top of l'Eixample, is named for the bicycle racetrack that used to be behind it. Despite the name, its focus now is pool and billiards in the back room, as well as necking on the lengthy, battered leather sofas. Its dilapidated art deco decor has seen better days—

probably before the Spanish Civil War (it opened in 1933)—but this contributes to the homey atmosphere. **Marcela** has been in the same family for five generations, and the long mahogany bar, stamped tin ceiling, crystal chandeliers, dusty bottles, and occasionally dustier clientele look as if they've been here that long as well. **El Xampanyet** is a postage-stamp spot in La Ribera (which was a very high-rent neighborhood of palaces in, say, 1492). The crowd and mood are as bubbly as the specialty *cavas* on the menu; the marble-topped tables and tilework depicting life in the Catalan countryside give it a cozy, shabbily genteel air. **Bar Hivernacle** occupies a soaring, turn-of-the-century, wrought-iron-and-glass greenhouse; the displays of tropical flora throughout make for excellent small talk when all else fails.

The art of the cocktail... One of the best and oldest (opened 1931) cocktail bars in town is the **Ideal.** Everyone looks as though they're rendezvousing with someone else's spouse and the low-volume music is strictly a backdrop for romantic murmurings. Scotch is the drink of choice and there's a wide range of single malts—that seems to fit with the plush, comfy chairs and English hunting prints adorning the walls. Surprisingly, the bartender also mixes a kick-ass mojito, the Cuban rum equivalent of a mint julep. The *best* place for mojitos, however, is **Boadas**. Here the daughter of the founder mixes them the same way her father did at the Floridita—Hemingway's old haunt in Havana—before he came to Barcelona and opened this art deco bar in 1933. At the **Gimlet** they make a good martini and—no surprise—an excellent gimlet. Its subdued and discreet elegance (the impassive, white-jacketed waiters excel at knowing their business but not yours) offers just the right atmosphere to get a little conspiracy or a love affair going. **Tres Torres**, in a renovated Art Nouveau mansion, is known for its potent martinis and it serves them with style; in warm weather the beautiful terrace is a wonderful place to play at being adult and civilized. **Marcela** is notable not only for its mix of expats, *guapo* (sexy) gay guys, and trendy local cognoscenti but also for its homemade variation of absinthe (yes, it's legal); here it's called *absenta*, which pretty much describes how you'll feel after belting a few back.

Designs for drinking... High as a kite on high-tech, **Network**, the early 1980s handiwork of architects Eduard Samsó and Alfredo Arribas, has a futuristic feel with gleaming metal everywhere and video monitors tuned to local television (or showing the occasional James Dean flick) on every table. The downstairs pool tables are the sole concession to the more typical bar scene. They must still be paying for the redecoration, as drinks are pricey. **Nick Havana**, also designed by Samsó, has a bank of 30 TV screens on one wall, striking but extraordinarily uncomfortable saddle-shaped chairs (courtesy of Philippe Starck), a huge pendulum swinging disconcertingly like an executioner's ax over the dance floor, and an ambience that calls for smart conversation (it even has a vending machine that dispenses paperback books). It's most crowded on weekends when a DJ's on duty playing house and techno. For a designer bar that harks back to the 1950s, check out **Velvet**, which has two horseshoe-shaped bars, a dance floor in between, and bathrooms done in industrial chrome. This fashionable place doesn't begin to get crowded until fashionably late (after midnight), when the wealthy and well-dressed show up in droves. A must-see, if only for its garish bad taste, is **Torres de Ávila**, a building in the Poble Espanyol with seven bars, each more outlandish than the next. The building and each of the bars were created by Javier Mariscal, designer of the Olympic logo, and architect Alfredo Arribas, who were in the forefront of the late eighties/early nineties designer boom. The theme is night and day, and it's filled with sun/moon/stars imagery. It's a tough place to carry on a conversation, but there's a sensational view from the rooftop terrace (open in summer). **Palau Dalmases** is designer in an entirely different sense: It's as if a tony Connecticut decorator had been transported to Ferdinand and Isabella's court. The opulent space, occupying the stables of a 17th-century palace, is awash in period splendor.

Strictly bubbly... Catalunya is a major producer of the sparkling wine known as *cava*, and Barcelona has more than its fair share of *xampanyerías*, bars devoted to the appreciation of this highly esteemed bubbly. **Xampu Xampany** is a pretty, relaxing place to learn the joys of *cava*, from brut (dry) to semi-brut to downright dulce (sweet). Compare the Tattinger's, available at about 16,250 ptas. ($125) a bottle, to the extremely fine local Torello Gran Reserva or Jaume de Codorniu, both of which run about 3,250 ptas. ($25) a bottle. At **La Cava del Palau**, you can enjoy the piano player tickling the ivories while the bubbly tickles your throat. Squeeze in at the bar **El Xampanyet** to watch the bartender pour the *cava* over his shoulder, aerating it as it falls into the glass. They also serve up a mean *sidra* (hard cider).

Painting the town pink... Daniella no longer owns Spain's first lesbian bar, **Daniel's Pub**, but the new management has kept it friendly, relaxed, and women-only. There's also still a pool table upstairs and a compact dance floor downstairs. Women can ignore the members-only sign; ring the bell and they'll let you in, along with cab drivers in leather and university professors in tweed. At **Bahia** all types, from hard-core butch to the girl next door, dance and chat the night away. It's a big, dark room with lots of wood, a good sound system, and ample room for boogying. While boys looking for bars won't want to miss the town of Sitges, one of the capitals of the gay map of Europe and just a half an hour south by train, Barcelona itself provides plenty of watering holes. **Dietrich Café** serves up strong drinks in a quiet, ample space with two bars, a glass atrium, and recorded jazz. It's a good choice for a first drink or two before going on to steamier venues. Just two doors down from the Dietrich, **Este Bar** is a narrow, crowded, smoky den. Most of the men preening at the long bar here are under 30. The house and hip-hop on the sound system render conversation moot. The decor, however, is *fabulous,* dahling; the best touches are the illuminated lavender columns (perfect for striking a pose) and the rotating art exhibits (often homoerotic). Don't miss the Creature from the Black Lagoon pinball machine or Jacqueline, the nickname for a machine in the rest room that dispenses panties. Neon glitz and potted plants provide an almost surreal contrast to the self-conscious Wild West–saloon decor (complete with swinging doors) at **New Chaps**. This spot caters to not-quite-young men on the make, who can get to know each other as the evening wears on in any of the bar's many nooks and crannies. **Marcela** is a relaxed, informal bar where young foreigners and older locals, straight and gay, mingle easily. Drag queens take over the tiny stage on Thursdays. Other nights there's no telling who may get up to perform. The folks behind Marcela opened **Ballet Blau**, an enormous space that packs them in for drag shows and surprisingly good live music weekends. The camp decor runs toward cherubs, gold floors and clouds painted everywhere.

Most pretentious... **Palau Dalmases** is proudly described by its owners as a "Baroque space and experi- ence" that "satisfies all five senses." It's just a tad over- done, with poor period paintings (of the "school of the school of" variety), stained glass and saints, gilt furnish- ings that feel as if they should be roped of with caution- ary "Don't Touch!" signs, and an almost stifling aroma of fresh flowers, potpourri, and fruit hanging in the air. Depending on your mood, it's either deliciously decadent or obnoxious. **Els Quatre Gats** served as a coffeehouse for young artists at the turn of the century. These days it caters to a classier set whose napkin doodles are more likely stock market tips. Aside from a couple of Picasso sketches, the "originals" on the walls were commissioned as reproductions by contemporary painters. It's a sacred watering hole that has been played up beyond reason; it is good for a drink but go somewhere else to eat.

What's on tapas?... Gourmands will be tempted by the sheer variety at **La Cervecería Catalana**. Seafood tapas are on one side of the room, and everything else, from small stuffed peppers to meatballs to cheeses on rounds of toast, is on the other. If you don't know the name of your selection, accompany the waiter back to the bar and point at it. The venerable **Gran Bodega** is an old-fash- ioned tapas bar with barrels of wine mounted on shelves and faded photos and chipped paintings of the neigh- borhood on the walls. Especially delectable are their *boquerones,* small fish marinated in vinegar, oil, garlic, and parsley. Anchovies are widely appreciated in Spain, and a good place at which to find out why is **El Xampanyet**, where they're served on crusty Spanish bread and washed down with hard cider or *cava.* The **Bar Celta**, close to the port, has a mind-boggling array of fresh seafood tapas on the bar and a crowd of young drinkers having a noisy good time. Try the delicious *pulpo gallego* (octopus Galicia-style), sprinkled with paprika, or the *raba* (deep-fried squid), and chase it all with the crisply acidic Galician white wines served in traditional ceramic jugs.

Get me a Guinness... The Quiet Man is about as Irish a pub as you'll find away from the Emerald Isle. It functions as something of an Irish cultural center, offering music, theater, and poetry readings in addition to the Guinness. At **Flann O'Brien's** you'll find English soccer on the telly, but also a wide selection of Irish beers and whiskies, live Irish folk music on Friday nights, and probably Van Morrison on the sound system on other nights. **Kitty O'Shea's** is pub culture at its most relaxed and amiable. Dark wood, roomy bar stools (with arm rests), a widescreen TV, and two large back rooms draw an international and largely yuppie crowd; you'll hear English, Castilian, and Catalan spoken here.

THE LOWDOWN

THE BAR SCENE

Note: Many bars and cafes open at 10am, serving coffee, crois-
sants, and breakfast sandwiches along with bar drinks. Bars
that cater to the late-late-night scene generally open at
8pm. Bars listed here are open daily unless otherwise noted.

Antiquari. Steeped in history and lively with conversation
today.... *Tel 315–31–09; Vaguer, 13; Jaume I metro stop.
Open until 2am.* **(see p. 157)**

Bahia. A relaxed atmosphere and a lesbian clientele.... *No
phone. Séneca, 12; Diagonal metro stop. Open 10pm–
3am.* **(see p. 161)**

Ballet Blau. Large, flamboyant gay bar specializing in drag shows
and cabaret.... *Tel 301–96–64. Junta de Comerç, 23; Liceu
metro stop. Open Tues—Sun 10pm–3am.* **(see p. 162)**

Bar Almirall. A bar from a bygone era, comfy and congenial....
*No phone. Joaquin Costa, 33; Universitat metro stop. Open
7pm–2:30am.* **(see p. 157)**

Bar Celta. Fresh seafood tapas, reasonably priced.... *Tel
315–00–06. Mercè, 16; Drassanes metro stop. Open
Mon–Sat until 1am; Sun until midnight.* **(see p. 162)**

Bar Glaciar. Funky bar with clientele that can charitably be
described as eclectic.... *Tel 302–11–63. Plaça Reial, 3;
Liceu metro stop. Open 9am–3am.* **(see p. 156)**

Bar Hivernacle. Circa 1900 greenhouse closes early
(10pm).... *Tel 268–01–77. Parc de la Ciutadella; Arc de
Triomf metro stop. Open 10am–10pm* **(see p. 159)**

Bar Kasparo. A great restful spot to nurse a drink and talk until midnight.... *Tel 302–20–72. Plaça Vinçenç Martorell, 4; Plaça Catalunya metro stop. Open daily 9am–midnight; closed Christmas season.* **(see p. 158)**

Bar London. Big and friendly; count on its being packed on weekends.... *Tel 318–52–61. Nou de la Rambla, 34; Drassanes metro stop. Open Tue–Sun 7pm–4am.*
(see p. 157)

Bar Pastis. For dedicated Francophiles.... *Tel 318–79–80. Santa Mónica, 4; Drassanes metro stop. Open Mon–Thur 7:30pm–2:30am; Fri; Sat until 3:30am.* **(see p. 157)**

Bar del Pi. For a drink before dinner; it's only open until 10pm.... *Tel 302–21–23. Plaça de Sant Josep Oriol, 1; Liceu metro stop. Open Mon–Sat 9am–11pm; Sun 10am–10pm.* **(see p. 156)**

Boadas. Right here off the Ramblas serving cocktails to a diverse group of regulars since 1933.... *Tel 318–95–92. Tallers, 1; Catalunya metro stop. Open Mon–Thur noon until 2am; Fri, Sat until 3; closed Sun.* **(see p. 159)**

Café de l'Opera. Perfect place to sip coffee, nurse a drink, read a paper, and watch the entire world go by.... *Tel 317–75–85. La Rambla, 74; Liceu metro stop. Open 8am–2am daily.* **(see p. 157)**

Casa Quimet. Gràcia's "guitar bar," where you're bound to hear one played.... *Tel 227–87–81. Rambla del Prat, 9; Fontana metro stop. Open until 2 am; closed Mon in Feb and Aug.*
(see p. 158)

La Cava del Palau. *Xampanyería* with a deservedly sterling reputation and tasty tapas to complement the *cava*.... *Tel 310–09–38. Verdaguer I Callis, 10; Urquinaona metro stop. Open until midnight.* **(see p. 161)**

La Cervecería Catalana. For just a bite. Or make a whole meal of their tapas.... *Tel 216–03–68. De Mallorca, 236; Passeig de Gràcia metro stop. Open until 1:30am.*
(see p. 162)

THE BAR SCENE INDEX

Daniel's Pub. Spain's oldest lesbian bar is still strictly for women only.... *Tel 209–99–78. Santa Peronella, 7–8; Fontana metro stop; buses 58, 64. Open Sun–Thur 8pm–2:30am; Fri–Sat 10pm–4am.* **(see p. 161)**

Dietrich Café. Early-evening spot for a predominantly gay crowd.... *No phone. Consell de Cent, 255; Universitat metro stop. Open until 3 am.* **(see p. 161)**

Els Quatre Gats. Turn-of-the-century ambience in a bar where Picasso's ghost still lingers.... *Tel 302–41–40. Montsió, 3-bis; Plaça Catalunya metro stop; bus Plaça Catalunya. Open Mon–Sat 8am–2 am, Sun 6pm–2am, closed Aug.*
(see pp. 156, 162)

Este Bar. The predominantly gay crowd here likes loud music.... *Tel 323–02–14 Consell de Cent, 257; Urgell metro stop; buses 14, 54, 58, 64. Open 7pm–2am.* **(see p. 161)**

Flann O'Brien's. The motto here is "A Pint of Plain Is Your Only Man.".... *Tel 201–16–06. Casanova, 264; buses 7, 14, 59, 66. Open until 2am.* **(see p. 163)**

Gran Bodega. Dark wood, tiled walls, marble-topped tables, and tapas.... *Tel 453–10–53. Valencia, 193; Passeig de Gràcia metro stop. Open until 1am.* **(see p. 162)**

Gimlet. Perfectly mixed drinks delivered to your table with style.... *Tel 310–10–27. Rec, 24; Jaume I metro stop. Open until 2:30am.* **(see p. 159)**

Ideal. A sedate, welcome break from the deafening noise of bars catering to younger crowds.... *Tel 453–10–28. De Aribau, 89; Universitat metro stop. Open until 2am.*
(see p. 159)

Kentucky. Shrine to the U.S. Navy attracts a varied crowd of tourists, hip locals, and yes, sailors from around the world.... *Tel 318–28–78. Arc del Teatre, 11; Drassanes metro stop. Open Mon–Sat 7pm–3am.* **(see p. 156)**

Kitty O'Shea's. An friendly uptown pub out by Pedralbes.... *Tel 280–36–75. Nau Santa María, 5; buses 6, 33, 66. Open until 2:30am.* **(see p. 163)**

Marcela. As comfortable as an old slipper, with a crowd that's mixed both in terms of nationality and sexual preference.... *No phone Sant Pau, 65; Liceu metro stop. Open Sun–Thur 9–2:30am, Fri–Sat 9–3am.* **(see pp. 159, 161, 162)**

Mirablau. The view is as good as they get, looking south over the city.... *Tel 418–58–79. Plaça del Dr. Andrea; tram Vía Blau. Open 11pm–4:30am.* **(see p. 158)**

Miramar. Drinks with a view from an historic hilltop.... *Tel 442–31–00. Avda. Miramar, S/9; bus 61. Open until 3am; closed Nov.* **(see p. 158)**

Network. A walk on the wild side of designer bardom.... *Tel 201–72–38. Avda. Diagonal, 616; buses 6, 7, 33, 34, 63. Open Sun–Thurs 10pm–2am; Fri–Sat 10pm–3am.* **(see p. 160)**

New Chaps. Not a mixed crowd–chaps only.... *Tel 215–53–65. Avda. Diagonal, 365; Diagonal metro stop. Open until 2:30am.* **(see p. 161)**

Nick Havana. One of the granddaddies of designer bars.... *Tel 215–65–91. Rosselló, 208; Diagonal metro stop. Open Mon–Fri 11pm–4am; Sat–Sun until 5am.* **(see p. 160)**

Palau Dalmases. Expensive, but you'll never find another place like it.... *Tel 310–06–73. Montcada, 20; Jaume I metro stop. Open until 2am; Sun until 11pm; closed Mon.* **(see pp. 160, 162)**

Port IMAX. A view to swoon for down at the port.... *Tel 225–18–36. Moll d'Espanya; Drassanes metro stop. Open until 11pm.* **(see p. 158)**

The Quiet Man. A little bit of Ireland in the Barri.... *Tel 412–12–19. Marquès de Barberà, 11; Liceu metro stop. Open until 2am.* **(see p. 163)**

Raval. Spacious surroundings and loquacious crowd.... *Tel 302–41–33. Doctor Dou, 19; Catalunya metro stop. Open Mon–Thur 8pm–2:30am; Fri–Sat 8pm–3am.* **(see p. 158)**

Salambo. Likely to fill up after a film has just let out at the cinema next door.... *Tel 218–69–66. Torrijos, 51; Joanic metro stop; buses 21, 39. Open until 2:30am.* **(see p. 158)**

Textil Cafè. Sipping a drink on the patio of this medieval palace you won't have any trouble remembering you're not in Kansas anymore.... *Tel 268–25–98. Montcada, 12–14; Jaume I metro stop. Open Tue–Sun until midnight, until 1am July and Aug.* **(see p. 157)**

Torres de Ávila. Seven bars in a tower in the Poble Espanyol.... *Tel 424–93–09. Avda. Marqués de Comillas. Espanya metro stop; bus 61. Open Thur–Sun 7pm–12:30am.* **(see p. 160)**

Tres Torres. A tasteful and relaxing ambience for sipping cocktails.... *Tel 203–98–99. Via Augusta, 300; Ferrocarril Les Tres Torres.* **(see p. 159)**

El Velòdrom. A neighborhood hangout in l'Eixample, just below the Avenida Diagonal.... *Tel 430–51–98. Muntaner, 213; Hospital/Clinic metro stop; buses 6, 7, 33, 58, 64. Open Mon–Thur 6pm–1:30am; Fri, Sat until 2:30am. Closed August.* **(see p. 158)**

Velvet. The aggressive decor and expensive drinks may not be for everyone, but it's a quintessential designer bar.... *Tel 217–67–14. Balmes, 161; buses 7, 16, 17. Open Sun–Thur 8pm–5am; Fri–Sat 8pm–6:30am.* **(see p. 160)**

El Xampanyet. Tapas, *cava*, and cider a few doors down from the Museu Picasso.... *Tel 319–70–03. De Montcada, 22; Jaume I metro stop. Open Tues–Sun noon–4pm; 6:30pm–11pm; closed August and Sun evenings.* **(see pp. 159, 161, 162)**

Xampu Xampany. A comfortable, cheerful bar with a *cava* fetish.... *Tel 265–04–83. Gran Vía de les Corts Catalanes. 702; Girona metro stop. Open Mon–Thur until 2am; Fri, Sat until 3.* **(see p. 160)**

the arts

Long integrated into
Europe's mainstream as
well as alternative arts
scenes, Barcelona has
always painted on a
broader cultural canvas
than the rest of Spain.

Indeed, the city has prided itself on being in the vanguard ever since Gaudí Domenech i Montaner, and Puig i Cadalfach revolutionized the *modernista* architectural movement (Barcelona's unique take on art nouveau) while Picasso sketched on napkins to pay his bar bills in the Barri Gòtic. Today, Barcelona continues to offer an exhilarating palette of avant-garde and bourgeois, conservative and controversial work.

While Barcelona's theater generally requires more Spanish or Catalan than the casual visitor can master or even muster, two superb theatrical cooperatives, **El Fura dels Baus** and **Els Comediants**, mount huge spectacles, often open-air, that render language practically superfluous. At their best, these draw the spectator into powerful public rituals filled with movement and color. They might perform anywhere around town, but El Fura dels Baus sometimes plays indoors, most often at **El Mercat de les Flors**. Formerly a sprawling flower market, this lovely building now has three theaters with good acoustics and sight lines. It is the principal venue for the summer arts festival, the **Grec** (see Down and Dirty), and for theater, dance, and music performances throughout the year. English-language dramatics, as well as poetry readings, are often staged at some of Barcelona's Irish pubs (though the quality is dubious.

There are several fine dance companies, which can be seen in **L'Espai de Catalunya, Sala Beckett**, or **El Mercat de les Flors**. For musical concerts, the most spectacular venue is the world's only *modernista* concert hall, the **Palau de la Música Catalana**. Everyone exclaims over Gaudí's goodies, but many aficionados consider his contemporary and rival, Lluís Domenech i Montaner, designer of the Palau as well as the remarkable Saint Paul Hospital, the greatest Catalan architect of them all. As you settle into your quite possibly stratospherically priced seat, let your eyes roam over the beautiful ceiling and the sculpted figures jutting out over the stage. The building's equally sumptuous exterior combines stained glass, brick, ornate stonework, and mosaics. Alas, in the design team's effort to make the Palau visually stimulating, they neglected the acoustics, which are dreadful. Nonetheless, the **Orquestra Simfónica Barcelona i Nacional de Catalunya** (Barcelona's symphony orchestra) plays here regularly, as do touring shows ranging from the Philadelphia Symphony Orchestra and the University Choir of the Balearic Islands to salsa troupes and top performers like Emmylou Harris and Ray Charles.

Until the reconstruction of the **Gran Teatre del Liceu** is completed, one of Europe's finest opera houses is dark, and Barcelona is without an opera season. In 1994 an errant welder's spark filled the sky above the Ramblas with smoke from the flaming Liceu. Word spread quickly and crowds gathered to watch as one of Barcelona's most emblematic buildings burned almost entirely to the ground. Before the ashes were cold, fund-raising for a new Liceu had begun. The old Liceu was a world-class venue—Spain's Placido Domingo, Italy's Luciano Pavarotti, and Catalonia's own Montserrat Caballé have all graced its stage, as has the work of Phillip Glass. The reopening is now scheduled for late 1998, but postponement has evolved into an annual ritual. You can always stop by and view the work in progress, but call ahead before your trip if you're thinking of making a night at the opera the centerpiece of your visit to Barcelona.

Tickets and Information

Tickets to most arts events are available from **Tel-Entrades** (tel 10–12–12). The best sources for current offerings are the daily newspapers. Both *La Vanguardia*, a family-owned newspaper in business for nearly 120 years, and *El País*, Spain's equivalent of the *New York Times*, include a section called *Cartelera*, which lists all the films that are showing with brief descriptions and a *versión original* (VO) notation where applicable (if the film is subtitled), as well as concert, exhibition, and theater information. The weekly *Guía del Ocio* also carries exhaustive listings. In English, there's the agenda section in the free monthly magazine *Barcelona Metropolitan*, which highlights live events. The **Centre d'Informació de la Virreina** (tel 301–41–98; La Rambla, 99; open 11am–2pm and 5pm–8pm, closed Sun) provides loads of information on what's going on throughout the year. And don't forget to check the kiosks found on many corners; they're plastered with announcements.

Timing

Museums are generally open from Tuesday through Saturday, until 8pm; some follow standard Spanish hours and close in the mid-afternoon, and many extend their hours during the summer. Cinemas are open daily.

The Lowdown

Up close and personal... After Franco died, an innovative and challenging dramatic form began to evolve in Barcelona. It is theater that blurs the lines between audience and actors by innovatively incorporating outdoor venues into the work and utilizing stunning visual effects to create a deep rite in which both thespian and spectator participate. The productions of the cooperative **Els Comediants**, active for over 25 years, contain little or no text—it's all image, mime, circus acrobatics, light, and sound, including mind-boggling fireworks. **La Fura dels Baus** is younger and has a distinctively more aggressive edge. The actors are likely to career at top speed through the crowd, and you may have to scramble out of the way. Their pieces are also strong and moving: emotionally prov-ocative, aurally and visually evocative. Expect anything in this theatrical bedlam from naked actors straddling your seat to power tools hammering away for sound effects.

The *theatah*... Slated to be open the end of 1997, the new **Teatre Nacional de Catalunya** occupies a remarkable building designed by architect Ricard Bofill, who also created Barcelona's airport. Melding solid classical Greek style with airy contemporary glass and light (think Pei meets the Parthenon), it holds two separate theaters, the larger of which will seat almost 1,000 people. You can see Shakespeare or Molière in Catalan here, or at the **Teatre Poliorama**. For Spanish versions, try **Teatre Tívoli**, which performs in a 1917 building designed by Miquel Madorell i Rius that features an iron and wood awning. New Catalan work is found at **Teatre Lliure**; current Spanish playwrights are featured at the **Villaroel**; and **Sala Beckett** offers experimental work from Catalonia and around Spain.

Light on their feet... Among Barcelona's internationally known modern dance companies are Gelabert-Azzopardi Companyia de Dansa (tel 416–00–68), led by Cese Gelabert; the four-woman, two-man Mudances (tel 430–87–63), whose most impressive works feature the dancers functioning as cogs of a well-oiled, highly structured machine; and Mal Pelo (tel 473–36–26), founded in 1989 by Pep Ramis and María Múñoz; the name means "bad hair," suggesting the troupe's wild, irreverent approach to dance, their best pieces treating bodies as mere objects that collide, merge, interact in specific spatial contexts such as city streets or crowded bars. To Barcelona's collective shame it does not have a ballet company, although touring troupes are frequently booked. To find out who is dancing where, call the companies or the **Associació dels Professionals de Dansa de Catalunya**. You can also try the usual dance venues, **L'Espai de Catalunya**, **El Mercat de les Flors**, and **Sala Beckett**, all known for avant-garde presentations.

Flocking to flicks... Both the latest Hollywood trash and the newest art-house sensation draw long lines, and some two dozen *versión original* (subtitled) films are usually showing on any given evening, most of them English or American. Barcelona's first multiple offerings of VO films came from **Verdi Cinemas**, a five-plex in Gràcia that still screens some of the most interesting offerings in town. It now competes with the six screens of the **Renoir-Les Corts Cinemas** in an uptown neighborhood, and 15 in the Olympic Village at **Icària-Yelmo Cinemas**, which has a more mainstream Hollywood bent. Even the Verdi has expanded, buying a building on the next block for the four-screen **Verdi Park Cinemas**. Many cinemas offer a midnight (actually, 12:30 or 12:45) show, likely to be a more obscure, offbeat flick. **Filmoteca de la Generalitat de Catalunya**, sponsored by the Catalan government, showcases older films in VO; you might be able to catch a little-known cycle of German films from the thirties, or something equally wonderful in English that you never get a chance to see.

In a classical mood... If the Orquestra Simfónica de Barcelona i Nacional de Catalunya is playing at the **Palau de la Música Catalana**, a decent seat can cost 8,100 ptas., and a good one at least 13,000, which is outrageous given the company's crashingly mediocre caliber (except when the program is Catalan music). A variety of other classical evenings are presented in the Palau, by both touring and resident groups, that offer both higher quality and greater value. Two or three times a year there are concerts on 17th-century instruments in **Santa María del Mar**, a beautiful, vaulting 14th-century church. They're not to be missed, especially if they feature Catalonia's Jordi Savall, the world's leading bass viol player.

Museum hopping... The **Museu Picasso**, located in a 15th-century palace, is the finest place in the world to see early Picasso, and we do mean early—from 1890, when Picasso was nine years old, to 1904, when he left Barcelona. There is also significant later work. The **Fundació Joan Miró's** beautiful building was designed by architect Josep Lluís Sert and opened in 1981. The collection displays a vast, comprehensive array of Miró's paintings, sculpture, and drawings, along with work by his well-known friends and contemporaries, such as Alexander Calder. The **Museu d'Art Contemporani de Barcelona (MACBA)** opened in 1995 in a great white whale of a building designed by U.S. architect Richard Meier; it houses a small, relatively well chosen post–World War II collection. The artwork is primarily Catalan, although there are a few decent Calders, Kiefers, and Lichtensteins, as well as intriguing temporary international installations. The **Museu Nacional d'Art de Catalunya** houses arguably the world's finest collection of 12th-century Romanesque art; highlights of the collection are murals painstakingly removed from the walls of churches in the Pyrenees. The museum is in the Palau Nacional (National Palace), which was built in 1929 and is an imposing space with a first-class view of the city below. It was recently renovated by noted Italian architect Gae Aulenti, who also did the Musée d'Orsay in Paris; the formerly gloomy halls are now filtered strategically with light that allows the magnificent artwork to glow. The museum supplies a guidebook in English. The **Centre Cultural de la Fundació la Caixa**, in a turn-of-the-century building designed by Josep Puig i Cadalfach in 1901, hosts an eclectic mix of traveling exhibits, such as works by New York photographer William Klein or Mexican painter Frieda Khalo, or a vast show of Tibetan Buddhist art.

Associació dels Professionals de Dansa de Catalunya. Clearinghouse open during the day for information on dance events citywide.... *Tel 268–24–73. Vía Laietana, 52, principal 12; Urquinaona metro stop.* **(see p. 173)**

Centre Cultural de la Fundació la Caixa. Traveling exhibits of world-class stature.... *Tel 458–89–07. Passeig de Sant Joan, 108; Verdaguer metro stop. Open Tue–Sat 11am–8pm.* **(see p. 174)**

Els Comediants. Has no phone or address and doesn't even issue tickets. Read the newspaper listings to find out when one of their infrequent (two or three times a year), eagerly anticipated performance events is taking place.
(see pp. 170, 172)

L'Espai de Catalunya. Often a venue for dance, it also offers live music and performance pieces. Operated by the Catalan government.... *Tel 414–31–33. Travessera de Gràcia, 63; buses 58, 64.* **(see p. 170, 173)**

Filmoteca de la Generalitat de Catalunya. You never can tell what VO movie will be playing.... *Tel 410–75–90. Avda. de Sarrià, 33; Hospital Clínic metro stop.*
(see p. 173)

Fundació Joan Miró. Leave yourself plenty of time to work your way through this exhaustive collection.... *Tel 329–19–08. Plaça Neptu, Parc de Montjuïc; bus 61 from the Avda. María Cristina in the Plaça Espanya. Open Tue, Wed, Fri, Sat 11am–7pm, Thur 10:30am–9:30pm.* **(see p. 174)**

El Fura dels Baus. See Els Comediants.

Gran Teatre del Liceu. A supremely elegant opera house, with chandeliers, red plush, and a superb stage before the disastrous fire of 1994, and once again, Barcelonans and opera lovers around the world hope, after the reconstruction.... *Tel 485–99–13. La Rambla, 67; Liceu metro stop.* **(see p. 171)**

Icària-Yelmo Cinemas. Its 15 screens must be showing *something* you want to see—if you like Hollywood, that is.... *Tel 221–75–85. Salvador Espriu, 61; Ciutadella-Vila Olímpica metro stop.* **(see p. 173)**

El Mercat de les Flors. What began as a huge flower market during the 1929 World's Fair has become host to drama, dance, and musical concerts.... *Tel 426–18–75. Lleida, 59; Espanya metro stop.* **(see pp. 170, 173)**

Museu d'Art Contemporani de Barcelona. You will either love or hate the controversial building, but the light-filled space creates optimal viewing for the artwork.... *Tel 412–08–10. Plaça dels Angels, 1; Catalunya metro stop. Open Tue–Sat noon–8pm.* **(see p. 174)**

Museu Nacional d'Art de Catalunya. Romanesque treasures in the huge, looming National Palace.... *Tel 423–71–99. Palau Nacional, Parc de Montjuïc; bus 61 from Avda. María Cristinas in the Plaça Espanya. Open Tue, Wed, Fri, Sat 10am–7pm, Thur until 9.* **(see p. 174)**

Museu Picasso. Ceramics, childhood scrawls, the Blue period, a few Cubist and later works: by no means a vast collection, but undeniably Picasso, and quite interesting.... *Tel 319–63–10. Montcada, 15–19; Jaume I metro stop. Open Tue–Sat 10am–8pm.* **(see p. 174)**

Palau de la Música Catalana. An art nouveau architectural fantasy and as unusual a setting for music as you'll find anywhere.... *Tel 268–10–00. Sant Francesc de Paula, 2; Urquinoana metro stop.* **(see pp. 170, 173)**

Renoir-Les Corts Cinemas. Subtitled films in a quiet uptown neighborhood.... *Tel 490–55–10. Eugeni d'Ors, 12; Les Corts metro stop.* **(see p. 173)**

Sala Beckett. A small, basement dance and theatre space in Gràcia.... *Tel 284–53–12. Alegre de Dalt, 55; Joanic metro stop.* **(see pp. 170, 173)**

Santa María del Mar. Soaring, slender eight-sided stone columns surround you in this church known for its concerts of 17th-century music.... *Tel 310–23–90. Plaça de Santa María; Jaume I metro stop. Open daily 8:30am–12:30pm and 4:30–8:10pm.* **(see p. 174)**

Teatre Lliure. Repertory company often credited with spurring the resurgence of Catalan drama.... *Tel 218–92–51. Montseny, 47; Fontana metro stop.* **(see p. 172)**

Teatre Nacional de Catalunya. Familiar plays in Catalan translation.... *Tel 246–00–41. Plaça de les Glories; Glories metro stop.* **(see p. 172)**

Teatre Poliorama. Currently in flux, but expected to be a primary venue for contemporary Catalan playwrights.... *Tel. 318–81–81. Rambla dels Estudis; Catalunuya metro stop.* **(see p. 172)**

Teatre Tívoli. Familiar plays in Spanish translation.... *Tel 412–20–63. Casp, 6; Urquinoana metro stop.* **(see p. 172)**

Verdi Cinemas. The best of serious, independent films play here in VO (with Spanish subtitles).... *Tel 237–05–16. Verdi, 32; Fontana metro stop.* **(see p. 173)**

Verdi Park Cinemas. Four more screens to handle the overflow from the Verdi, and a similar selection of films.... *Tel 217–88–23. Torrijos, 49; Fontana metro stop.* **(see p. 173)**

Villaroel. Contemporary Spanish theater, in Spanish.... *Tel 451–12–34. Villaroel, 87; Universitat metro stop.* **(see p. 172)**

THE ARTS / INDEX

10 hanging out

If even the industrious locals manage to spend a substantial part of every day and night refining the art, then hanging out is absolutely obligatory for visitors. People here make time to enjoy their city as conscientiously as they work, eat, and sleep. As a result, Barcelona is full of world-class spots for pursuing life's more idle pleasures, whether that be commandeering a choice seat at Las Ramblas or Marina sidewalk cafe, or wandering the torturous streets of the Barri Gòtic, whose churches (like the Cathedral and the majestic Catalan Gothic Santa María del Mar), palaces (the two-block-long Carrer Montcada boasts six in stately procession), and ravishing plazas are usually brilliantly illuminated by man or moon. Best of all, Barcelona is compact: you can easily walk from the Barri Gòtic to slightly ramshackle Barceloneta and its fishing boats as brightly colored as a child's finger painting to the ultramodern Port Olímpic complex. The city's personality changes within a matter of minutes. Any medieval Barcelona alley could open onto a *modernista* masterpiece or chrome-and-black glass tower resembling a Vuarnet lens.

Ever practical, Barcelonans have not overlooked an important, though rarely discussed, aspect of hanging out—finding a way to answer the call of nature without having to go all the way back to your hotel or buy something you don't want in a bar. For just 25 ptas., you can find relief in one of central Barcelona's many unisex green plastic cubicles, which are fitted out with the essential plumbing and identifiable by the familiar "WC." Unfortunately, they are not wheelchair-accessible, and, especially around Las Ramblas and the Barri Gòtic, hanging out occasionally takes on another meaning entirely: Barcelona has its lunatic fringe just like any other city.

HANGING OUT ☾ INTRODUCTION

Letting life pass you by... To view the passing
parade of humanity in its widest possible permutations,
you can't beat the mile-long pedestrian promenade along
La Rambla between the Monument à Colom and the
Plaça de Catalunya. Here you'll be distracted by human
sculptures being taunted by biker chicks who look as if
they've been freshly discharged from a mental ward, or by
elegant couples in their seventies walking by arm in arm,
oblivious. So popular is this diversion that Barcelonans
have coined a term, *ramblejant,* to describe the experience. You can always amble among the rambling crowd;
if you want a seat—and La Rambla offers some wonderful ringside seats—you have to know where to look. For
cafés with outdoor seating, head for the lower end by
the Monument a Colom; in the middle, the railing of the
stairs leading into the Metro at Liceu provides a perch.
At the upper end, near the Plaça de Catalunya, just below
a permanent knot of old men who stand around day and
night arguing politics, sports, and philosophy, are two
rows of aluminum chairs lining either side of the boulevard. Sit down in one of the chairs, and after a while a fellow will saunter over; give him 40 ptas. (less than 25
cents) and you have just rented that chair until hell freezes
over, or until you decide to get up and move on, whichever
comes first. After 10pm the man who collects the money
goes home and you can take a seat for free.

   To the north of La Rambla is the **Plaça Reial**, in the
old city, with remarkable lampposts designed by Antoni
Gaudí. The benches are crowded, but it's worth trying to
find a seat to watch the streams of international travelers
and local ne'er-do-wells pass through (it's a favorite
pick-up place for quasi-gigolos with slicked-back hair
and tufts of fur artfully playing peekaboo above their silk

shirts). Off the southern side of La Rambla, in the Raval, the **Biblioteca de Catalunya** has a lovely courtyard with orange trees and low stone walls (open until 8pm). Enter from Calle de l'Hospital, 56. Just about anywhere along the port or the beaches is prime territory for relaxing; the benches behind the **Maremagnum** offer a view across the harbor.

Best views (for free)... The city is spread out below you from many points on the mountain of **Montjuïc**; the **Palau Nacional** in the Parc de Montjuïc (Espanya metro stop) makes the most stunning backdrop. To avoid the long, somewhat strenuous uphill walk you can take the number 61 bus from Avenida María Cristina near the metro entrance at Plaça Espanya. A terrific city view is also to be had from the **Parc Güell**, the park designed by Gaudí (open May–Aug until 9pm; April, Sept until 8pm; until 6pm the rest of the year). But the city takes a backseat to the park itself, a marvelously mutant Disneyland. The approach, through spindly, spidery colonnades resembling stone palm trees that seamlessly interlace with the hillside and culminate in a forest of wildly contorted Doric columns (exemplifying Gaudí's brilliant fusion of natural and architectural forms), is spectacular, as is the broken mosaic work adorning the benches. If you are with friends who have a car (we hope you haven't been driving around town yourself—see Down and Dirty), you may want to visit the range of hills just to the north and west of Barcelona, the **Collserola**, via any of the three main roads that cross the it, carretera Sarrià, car retera Sant Cugat, or carretera Horta. Barely outside town, you'll start seeing pull-offs from which you can admire the lights of Barcelona below. When you're ready to turn your back on the city, the sea offers its own stunning vistas. You can enjoy the view from above at **Miramar**, the lookout point facing the sea atop Montjuïc. Or take a **waterfront walk**, starting at the Maremagnum (Drassanes metro stop) and heading north past the Port IMAX, behind the Palau del Mar, and following the Passeig Don Joan de Borbò down to the sea, where a mile and a quarter of beach begins. Head toward the huge copper fish by sculptor Frank Gehry; it gleams even at night, reflecting the lights from the Hotel Arts behind it.

HANGING OUT ⏐ THE LOWDOWN

Best views (for a fee)... Gaudí's **Temple Expiatori de la Sagrada Familia** may be unfinished, but it still offers some of the best views of Barcelona that money can buy. There is a fee of 750 ptas. to enter the church, and another of 125 ptas. to ride an elevator up to nearly the top of one of the twisted spires, from which you have a marvelous—though vertiginous—view of the city. The intrepid can climb further up the tower. You can walk back down the narrow winding steps, stopping for various panoramas along the way, or take the elevator back to ground level. Hours vary throughout the year, so it's best to call ahead (tel 455–02–47; de Mallorca, 401; Sagrada Familia metro stop). The tram from Plaça Doctor Andreu brings you to a funicular (250 ptas. round trip; last one heads up at 9:45pm), which takes you up the mountain of **Tibidabo** for capacious views of the city and, in good weather, out to sea. If the view from the ground on Tibidabo isn't enough for you, continue in the glass elevator up the front of the **Torre de Collserola**, a communications tower built for the 1992 Olympics that offers expansive views over miles of Catalunya (tel 211–79–42; 350 ptas.; elevator operates until 8pm). From June into September, the city-and-waterfront view from the **Monument à Colom**, erected for the 1888 International Exposition at the foot of the Ramblas, is accessible until 9pm; during the rest of the year, hours vary (tel 302–52–34; Drassanes metro stop; admission: 250 ptas. for adults, 125 ptas. for those over 65 or under 14).

Adult toys... Franchised sex shops catering to heterosexual fantasies and fetishes, like **Magic America** (tel 451–79–70; Avda. Paral.lel, 52–54; open until midnight) and **Blue Box** (tel 487–24–55; Aragon, 249), are scattered all over town. They sell everything from videotapes to vibrators and have booths for video watching. Gay men may find their toys of choice at **Sextienda** (tel 318–86–76; Rauric, 11; open Mon–Sat until 8:30pm). See also Down and Dirty.

To the baths... Especially after the clubs let out, gay men gather at the **Sauna Casanova** (tel 323–78–60; Casanova, 57) and **Sauna Thermas** (tel 325–93–46; Diputació, 46). They are open around the clock on weekends and until 5:30am during the week. You're charged for drinks when you leave, and it's a good idea to bring your own condoms, since management usually runs out by 11pm.

Designing evenings... The two best shopping streets for designer apparel, accessories, and home furnishings are **Passeig de Gràcia** and the **Rambla Catalunya**, where you will find fashionable clothiers like **Adolfo Domínguez** (tel 487–36–87), Catalan clothing and shoe designer **Toni Miró's** store, **Groc** (tel 215–01–80), **Loewe's** (tel 216–04–00) for leather goods, and **Vinçon** (tel 215–60–50), the local mecca for designer furniture and kitchen and bath wares. Close by, **BD Ediciones de Diseño** (Mallorca, 291), offers reproductions of furniture designed by artists from Gaudí to Ricard Bofill, Oscar Tusquets, and Javier Mariscal, designer of the Olympic logo.

Browsing for books... After you buy a book from **Laia Llibreria's** respectable stock of titles in English, you can read it upstairs over a cuppa java at the **Café Laia**; in nice weather you can even sip on the terrace (tel 301–73–10, Pau Claris, 85; Urquinaona metro stop; bookstore open until 9pm, café until 1am). Barcelona's centrally located women-oriented bookstore, **Prolèg** (tel 319–24–25; Dagueria, 13; Jaume I metro stop; open Mon–Sat until 8pm), stocks English books, non-touristy postcards, and cool-to-kitsch original jewelry; the friendly owner will invariably direct you to the changing art exhibits in back. **Altaïr** (tel 454–29–66; Balmes, 71; open Mon–Sat until 9pm) specializes in travel and anthropology in English and Spanish, including guides to just about every corner of the world.

Browsing for newspapers and magazines... All-night news junkies should head for **La Rambla**, where the kiosks stay open around the clock and sell a good variety of foreign newspapers and magazines (as well as porn that's legible in most any language). Also stocking English magazines, though fewer of them, are the **VIPs** (tel 317–48–05; Rambla de Catalunya, 7 and Comte de Borrell, 308; open until 2am). If you don't mind reading last week's *New Yorker* and prefer a free copy, you can lounge over it at the **Institut de Estudis Nort Americans**, known among *angloparlantes* simply as the North

American Institute (tel 200–27–11 Vía Augusta, 123; open until 9pm).

Old and older... The streets branching out of the Plaça del Pi are full of antique shops, most with equally aged owners who haggle ferociously; try **Llibreria Trallero** (tel 315–90–54; de la Palla, 33; open until 8:30) for anything appropriately yellowed or peeling, from maps to books, furniture, prints, and assorted curiosities. For ceramics try **Arturo Ramón** (tel 302–59–0; de la Palla, 25; open until 8pm); **Alberto Grasas** (tel 442–94–71; de la Palla, 10 bis; open until 8pm) has an interesting selection of furniture, paintings, and porcelain. There's an antiques market every Thursday in the Plaça del Pi that wraps up around dark. In the Raval, **L'Arca de l'Avia** (tel 302–15–98; Banys Nous, 20; open until 8:30pm) specializes in antique cottons, linens, and silks, and **Galuchat** (tel 487–58–55; Valencia, 261; open until 9pm) in l'Eixample is full of kitschy oddities.

Music of the night... The **Virgin Megastore** (tel 412–44–77; Passeig de Gràcia, 16; open Mon–Thur until 9pm; Fri, Sat until 10:30) is just what the name promises—two floors of CDs, cassettes, and crowds. **Planet Music** (tel 451–42–88; Mallorca, 214; open Mon–Sat until 9pm), in the heart of l'Eixample, has a wide selection of jazz and global music, with less of a warehouse atmosphere and more helpful personnel. Another music source is the branch of the French giant **FNAC** (tel 444–00–00; Avda. Diagonal, 545–557; open Mon–Sat until 9:30pm) in the L'Illa mall.

Killing time between clubs... Insomniacs, people who work the night shift, and committed club-goers rely on **Depaso** (tel 454–58–46; Muntaner, 14) for basic groceries, sandwiches, records, newspapers, little gift items, and other essentials. In case you need a taste of home, there are **7-11s**; most are out on the highways, but one is fairly centrally located (tel 318–88–63; Plaça Urquinaona). Electronics and film, as well as newspapers and magazines, are at the **VIPs** (see above) and **Drugstore David** (tel 200–47–30; Tuset, 19–21, just above Avda. Diagonal; open Mon–Sat until 5am, Sun to midnight); David's also has food and wine.

11

late night dining

Given the workaholic
tendencies of the local
populace, Barcelona
restaurants are often
glorified forums for
conducting business, albeit
in convivial settings.

Indeed, the seating plans at the trendier yuppieterias are as strategic as at a White House dinner. But the dignified, even dour, faces the natives put on belie their lusty earthiness. Food, dining out, even digestion, all play integral roles in the Catalan lifestyle. A popular Christmas decoration unique to Catalonia is the *caganer*, a figure of a peasant squatting to take a dump right by little baby Jesus, displayed even in the most conservative suburban crèches. It's no surprise, then, that a favorite local saying is "Eat well, crap hard, and guffaw at death."

From the American standpoint, all Spaniards dine unfashionably late. Even the most family-oriented Barcelona restaurant opens its doors no earlier than 9pm and serves food through midnight on a weeknight, until 1 or 2am on weekends. You may wonder why they wait so long when the meals are invariably appetizing, even at the humblest corner café; Catalan cuisine is greatly underrated. Catalonians themselves take deep delight and a justifiable pride in their native fare. It draws from a variety of meats and seafood, as well as fresh vegetables, all prepared with liberal quantities of excellent olive oil. Many dishes utilize one of three basic, delectable sauces: *sofregit* (fried diced tomato and onion), *all i oli (garlic mayonnaise)*, and *samfaina* (peppers, onions, eggplant, tomatoes, and garlic). There are great seasonal specialties like *calçots*, a big leek served with thick, goopy, garlicky almond paste, available November through March. You dip the leek in the paste and stuff it in your mouth—you'll need the bib they bring with the dish. Also typical is the wonderful, simple *pa amb tomaquet*, a piece of bread rubbed with half a tomato, and for dessert, **crema catalana**, the Catalan version of flan, with a burnt sugar crust. Though the 1992 Olympics popularized cuisines from around the globe, Barcelona remains unexpectedly deficient in gourmet French, Italian, or Chinese restaurants. You're unlikely to care, though, given the richness of the local and other Spanish regional fare. For information on etiquette, tipping, and Spanish wines, see Madrid Late Night Dining.

The Lowdown

Catalan home cooking... The best place to go for *calçots* is indisputably **El Glop**, an informal, family-style Gràcia institution. Don't be put off by the name, which means "the sip," though unabashed slurping is fairly common here. The oldest restaurant in Barcelona is, of course, classically Catalan: **Can Culleretes** began serving meals in 1786, and the maze-like interior is plastered with ancient copper pots, pottery, posters, and photos attesting to this spot's enduring popularity. If the combination of spinach, pine nuts, and raisins sounds appealing, try *espinaca catalana*, a traditional appetizer. Another specialty is the thick, sultry *civet de porc senglar* (wild boar stew), which seems to have been bubbling for days; the luscious meat falls off the bone. There's no mistaking the common ownership or tourist trade appeal of **Les Quinze Nits**, **L'Hostal de Rita**, and **La Fonda**. They all have the same light airy design and strikingly similar menus. Their collective reputation for delicious food imaginatively prepared, combined with reasonable prices and a no-reservation policy, explains the long lines jostling and jockeying to get in. Deep in the old city, the whitewashed walls and oak floors of **Agut d'Avignon** set the tone for truly gourmet Catalan fare. The duck with figs entrée is particularly notable, as is the wild boar with strawberry sauce. For an innovative twist on traditional Catalan, head up to the airy, glass-roofed second floor of **Tragaluz**, where chef Joan Ferrer blends culinary delights from southern France with those of Catalonia. Regular entrées include pigs feet stuffed with ground pork and herbs; and quail with a light soy-based sauce and fresh asparagus.

From the sea... A quintessential Barcelonan gastronomic experience consists of grabbing a quick, cheap, stand-in-the-street-and-eat meal from one of the vendors' stalls facing the beach under the walkway by the Platja Passeig Maritim. The squid and mussels, prepared right before your eyes (and under your nose), are a specialty. The somewhat fussily tasteful anteroom at the premier Basque eatery **Beltxenea** looks like a 19th-century parlor (it is); in warm weather, the pebble garden at the rear is one of the city's choicest outdoor seating areas. House specialties include marvelous melon and lobster salad and baked hake. **Can Ros** is your basic Barceloneta dive, both serviced by and catering to the neighborhood's seagoing families; fresh seafood is served in a brisk ambience. Don't miss the *mejillones a la marinera*, made with tangy, small wild mussels, rather than the milder farm-raised variety. At **Can Costa** they've been cooking seafood for more than 70 years: the *chipirones* (baby squid) are flash-fried to perfection, and the *fideuá de peix* puts a twist on the classic shellfish paella, substituting noodles for rice. Traditionally, paella, that marvel of saffroned rice, seafood, chicken, sausage, and vegetables originally created in Valencia, is eaten at midday, but a good paella hits the spot anytime, and **Set Portes**, between Las Ramblas and Barceloneta, keeps turning them out until 1am. This combination bistro-brasserie really does have seven doors—and has logged over a century and a half at the same location. Despite being steeped in ambience (and crawling with tourists of the sort who ask the pianist to play "Don't Cry for Me, Argentina"), the prices haven't gotten too steep.

Getting your greens... Barcelona is hardly a vegetarian city; people here love their meat and fish. There are, however, a handful of good vegetarian restaurants and several others that include a good selection of vegetarian entrées on their menus. In the latter group is **La Buena Tierra**, in a charming old Gràcia house with a peaceful garden in back. Their *canelons del bosc* (cannelloni with wild mushrooms), is luscious, the delicate flavor of the mushrooms never drowned out by the hearty sauce. **Govinda** attracts an international crowd for its all-vegetarian northern Indian food and large salad bar; it's popular with purists, Mormons, Shiite Muslims, reformers, and teetotalers of all stripes because neither alcohol nor coffee are served. Dishes such as *sapnam* curry, cooked with peas and a bland cheese made on the premises, are tasty without being too spicy. **Illa de Gràcia** serves an excellent, inexpensive, all-vegetarian menu. Their specialty is *crep illa de Gràcia*, made with mushrooms, cream, and pepper. You can order beer or wine with your meal, a rarity in vegetarian restaurants here. You can also smoke cigarettes, or simply bask in the secondhand haze from the couple at the next table.

Where tourists and Barcelonans mix... It's a good sign when a place can draw both locals and visitors: the cuisine meets local standards yet the atmosphere doesn't scream "Yankee, Go Home!" A trio of Catalan restaurants—**Les Quinze Nits**, **La Fonda**, and **L'Hostal de Rita** (under the same management)—all offer menus in English, Castilian, and Catalan for the United Nations clientele that mingles in their airy, light-filled rooms. At **El Glop**, good food and an easygoing ambience do the trick. Vegetarians seem to relate well the world over and the comfortable, calming surroundings of **La Buena Tierra** bring foreigners and locals together.

Where they don't... At **Set Portes**, the people at the next table are more likely to be speaking German, French, English or Japanese than Catalan, but the seafood-oriented menu is unlikely to disappoint anyone. **Beltxenea** draws wealthy tourists and business travelers on expense accounts, their waistbands happily expanding as their wallets contract. The atmosphere may be stuffy, but after stuffing yourself with the finest Basque food in town, you won't care.

A bowl of miso soup... The large number of Japanese tourists and businesspeople in Barcelona—who venerate the city's patron architect, Antoni Gaudí, and his sinuous forms—has spawned a growing crop of Japanese restaurants. **Koyuki** has only six tables and a sushi bar; if you don't make a reservation, you could easily get socked by one sake too many as you wait, watching the chef deftly slice the sublime sashimi. That Nippon nipping should help you appreciate the long room a few steps down from the eating area; it's lined with shelves of Japanese comic books, which are sourly scanned by the lonely, mostly male clientele. A few blocks away, **Yu** offers fresh fare at fair prices. For starters try the mouthwatering *gyoza* (dumplings); of the sushi, the *maki* (raw tuna) is a standout. You can start or make a meal with the renowned vegetable tempura and other little dishes such as *kusiyaki* (grilled kebobs) at **Tragaluz**, a restaurant with a split personality: Japanese tapas on the first floor and Mediterranean cuisine upstairs.

Food with a view... There's nothing like dining by the water on a warm evening—especially along the long shoreline of which Barcelonans are justifiably proud. At **La Gavina**, behind the Palau de Mar, you can feast on seafood on a terrace facing the yacht basin. The house specialties are a *fideu* with clams and tiny octopi, and *navajas* (razor clams; it also means "pocket knife"—though the clientele is hardly the roustabout type). **Can Costa** also offers an aquatic view—this one of the harbor—when the weather's nice enough to sit outside. At the tiny **Bar Pinocho**, you can watch the hustle and bustle of the Boqueria market swirl around you; the local color (not to mention the sounds and smells) is vivid indeed. It's the ideal spot for breakfast before bed (try *pa amb tomaquet*), as vendors of virtually anything you can imagine cooking—and some things you can't—prepare for another day.

Late, late... If you're hungry at 2am, drop by the **Café Arnau** on the Avenida Parallel, next door to the Teatro Arnau. If you arrive after 3 and the metal gate is down, try ringing the bell—they'll usually let you in. The menu is standard pub grub (mostly sandwiches), but its location in Barcelona's theater district draws a clientele out of "Damon Runyon à la Catalonia." If you're on your way home after a long night out and the sun is already up, head for **Bar Pinocho**. This hole in the wall with six stools in the Boquería marketplace by the Ramblas is a favorite for breakfast after marathon partying. Or, if you find yourself at the Polyester (see The Club Scene) in need of a second wind, you can refuel with sandwiches and regain your senses at **Midnight Express**. Conveniently located above the club, this beautifully restored Art Deco café in Barcelona's cavernous train station conveniently opens at 5am on weekends, as the thrashing bodies at Polyester are in full swing.

$$$$	over 7,500 ptas.	more than $60
$$$	4,500–7,500 ptas.	$35–$60
$$	2,500–4,500 ptas.	$20–$35
$	under 2,500 ptas.	Less than $20

Prices reflect average price for three courses per person; drinks and tip are not included.

Agut d'Avignon. Expensive, and worth every peseta.... *Tel 302–60–34. Trinitat, 3; Liceu metro stop. Open until 11:30pm. $$$$* **(see p. 187)**

Bar Pinocho. Simple Catalan fare in a space scarcely bigger than the surrounding market stalls.... *Tel 317–17–31. Stall 67–68, Boquería Market; Liceu metro stop. Open Mon–Sat 6:30am–4pm. No credit cards. $* **(see p. 190)**

Beltxenea. Haute Basque-style seafood in the heart of a l'Eixample neighborhood.... *Tel 215–30–24. Mallorca, 275; Passeig de Gràcia metro stop. Open until 11:30pm. MC not accepted. $$$$* **(see pp. 188, 189)**

La Buena Tierra. Vegetarian food in a relaxing atmosphere.... *Tel 219–82–13. Encarnació, 56; Joanic metro stop. Open Mon–Sat until midnight. DC not accepted. $$* **(see pp. 188, 189)**

Café Arnau. Where theater people go for a bite after the last curtain call.... *Tel 329–99–24. Avda. Parallel, 62; Parallel metro stop. Open until 3am or later; closed Wed. No credit cards. $* **(see p. 190)**

Can Costa. After stuffing yourself with paella, try to find room for a homemade pastry to finish the meal.... *Tel 221–*

59–03. *Passeig Don Joan de Borbò, 70; Barceloneta metro stop. Open Mon–Sat until 11:30pm. AE, DC, MC not accepted.* $$ **(see pp. 188, 190)**

Can Culleretes. Authentic Catalan cuisine in a venerable restaurant that combines quality, ambience, and value.... *Tel 317–30–22. Quintana, 5; Liceu metro stop. Open Tue–Sat until 11pm; closed July 1–21.* $$ **(see p. 187)**

Can Ros. Seafood taken very seriously.... *Tel 221–45–79. Almirall Aixada, 7; Barceloneta metro stop. Open until midnight; closed Sun, Wed. DC, MC not accepted.* $$
(see p. 188)

La Fonda. Sister restaurant of Les Quinze Nits and L'Hostal de Rita.... *Tel 301–75–15. Escudellers, 10; Drassanes metro stop. Open until 11:30pm.* $ **(see pp. 187, 189)**

La Gavina. Moderately expensive seafood with a tranquil view.... *Tel 221–05–95. Moll del Diposit, by the Palau de Mar; Barceloneta metro stop. Open until 11pm.* $$$
(see p. 190)

El Glop. Specializes in what you might eat in any middle-class Catalan's home, and that's who your fellow diners will be.... *Tel 213–70–58. Sant Lluís, 24; Joanic metro stop. Open Tue–Sat until 1am. AE, DC not accepted.* $$
(see pp. 187, 189)

Govinda. One of the city's older vegetarian eateries.... *Tel 318–77–29. Plaça Vila de Madrid, 4–5; Catalunya metro stop. Open Tue–Sat until 11:45pm.* $ **(see p. 188)**

Illa de Gràcia. Super-low prices may help make up for the smoke in your eyes.... *Tel 238–02–29. Sant Domenec, 19; Fontana metro stop. Open Tue–Sun until midnight. AE not accepted.* $ **(see p. 189)**

Koyuki. The owner is brusque and efficient, and the Japanese food top-notch.... *Tel 237–84–90. Córcega, 242; buses 58, 64. Open Tue–Sun until 11:30.* $$ **(see p. 189)**

L'Hostal de Rita. Same decor, same ambience, same tourists-and-locals crowd as Les Quinze Nits and La Fonda—and

the same great Catalan fare.... *Tel 487–33–60. Aragó, 279; Passeig de Gràcia metro stop. Open until 11:30pm. $*
(see pp. 187, 189)

Les Quinze Nits. One of three co-owned Catalan restaurants (with La Fonda and L'Hostal de Rita) that all have the same (good) food and feel—this is the one with outdoor seating.... *Tel 317–30–75. Plaça Reial, 6; Liceu metro stop. Open until 11:30pm. $*　　　**(see pp. 187, 189)**

Midnight Express. For a morning pick-me-up after a night of head-banging, or when you're on your way to catch a train.... *Tel 310–14–78. Estació de França, Avda. Marqués de la Argentera; Barceloneta metro stop. Opens Mon–Fri at 6:45am; Sat, Sun at 5am. No credit cards. $*
(see p. 190)

Set Portes. A seafood institution, in operation since 1836.... *Tel 319–29–50. Passeig Isabel II. 14; Barceloneta metro stop. Open until 1am. $$$*　　　**(see pp. 188, 189)**

Tragaluz. Two in one: Japanese tapas on the ground floor, and full Mediterranean-inspired dinners upstairs.... *Tel 487–01–96. Passeig Concepció, 5; Passeig de Gràcia metro stop. Open until midnight. $$$*
(see pp. 187, 190)

Yu. Elegantly simple Japanese in l'Eixample.... *Tel 451–94–46. De Valencia, 204; Universitat metro stop; buses 54, 58, 64, 66. Open Mon–Sat until 12:30am. $$*　　　**(see p. 189)**

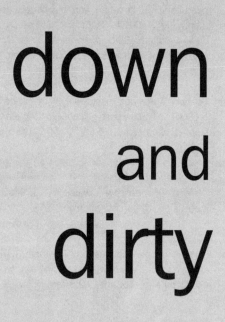

down
and
dirty

Airport... **Aeroport del Prat** was entirely renovated for the 1992 Olympics. The new international terminal, an impressive expanse of glass and marble, was designed by noted Catalan architect Ricardo Bofill. The currency exchange offices are open until 10:45pm. It's a 20-minute, 2,000-ptas. cab ride to the city, or you can take one of the buses that leave every 15 minutes. The last one leaves the airport for the city at 11pm, and the last one from the city (Pl. Catalunya) leaves at 10:45pm.

All-night pharmacies... Let's hope you won't need one, but in a city where even vitamins and aspirin have to be bought in a pharmacy, it's best to be prepared. As in Madrid, the pharmacies that are open after 9pm rotate weekly by law. Every pharmacy posts a list of the week's late-night locations by its entrance; the list is also printed in the daily newspapers.

Babysitters... If your hotel can't arrange child care, you do have some alternatives. **Cangur Serveis** (tel 487–80–08; Aragón, 227) will provide someone by the hour (800 ptas.) or all night (6,000 ptas.), and they employ a number of English speakers. They also have a day-care center at their central office. **Cinc Serveis** (tel 412–56–76; Pelai, 11, 5-C; tel 908–599–700 for 24-hour service) also has baby-sitters available around the clock, and some speak good English. After 9pm the rate is about 1,100 ptas. an hour; during the day it's cheaper.

Car rental... Driving a car in Barcelona is just about as pleasant—and almost as expensive—as having a root canal, unless you plan on exploring the surrounding Costa Brava. A small European car costs about 9,000 ptas. a day, 21,000 ptas. for a weekend, or 50,000 ptas. for a week. Be over 21 and have a driver's license from somewhere. Rental companies include **Hertz** (tel 217–80–76, fax 237–29–20; Tusset, 10); **Vanguard** (tel 439–38–20, fax 410–82–71; Londres, 31); **Avis** (tel 487–87–54, fax 487–20–50) with five offices; **Europcar** (tel 439–84–03, fax 419–38–17) with two locations; and **Thrifty** (tel 430–90–71, fax 439–43–47; Avda. Sarrià, 32).

Chauffeurs... If cabs don't appeal to you, go ahead and hire a chauffeur-driven car from **Travanco Eurorental** (tel 439–25–38; Viladomat, 212); **Julià Car** (tel 431–11–00; Santa Eulàlia, 176); or **Gestvi** (tel 490–97–63; Gran Vía Carles III, 12). Like to wrap a limousine around your chauffeur? Try **Barcelona Limousine Service** (tel 247–

BARCELONA ⟨ DOWN AND DIRTY

06–99; Valencia, 455); **International Limousine** (tel 448–39–39; Avda. Diagonal, 661); or **R & M Limousines Barcelona** (tel 418–05–50; Plaça Ramón Godón, 5).

City information... For 140 ptas. you can dial **010** Monday through Saturday until 10pm and ask almost any question about Barcelona you can imagine, from where to go to church to where to have an abortion to who is playing what where on any given evening. You'll have to do it in Spanish or Catalan, however, as they don't offer English speakers.

Emergencies... For medical emergencies call the **Barcelona Medical Centre** (tel 290–68–59), open 24 hours specifically for foreigners. For an **ambulance** call **061** or **300–20–20**. To report a **fire** call **080**. For the *Policía Nacional* call **091** and for the **municipal police**, **092**. **Turisme-Atención** (tel 301–90–60; La Rambla, 43) is a police station specifically for tourists; an English-speaking officer is always available. If your passport is lost or stolen, immediately report it to the nearest police station and to your consulate. The **U. S. Consulate** (tel 280–22–27; Pg. Reina Elisenda Montcada, 23) is only open until 5pm but has an after-hours emergency number (tel 414–11–00); if you leave your number someone should call you back within half an hour.

Festivals and special events...

February: **Carnestoltes** (Carnival) is celebrated with all the traditional pomp and extravagance as it is elsewhere. It's most notable for several Barcelonan traditions that recur at other festivals throughout the year. One is the *castell,* or human tower. For some inexplicable reason, clubs have formed to compete to see who can create the highest building of flesh and sinew and design the most elaborate costumes. Other typical sights include the fantastic, phantasmagorical *gegants* (giants), 15-feet-tall figures made of papier-mâché and wood, and *capgrossos,* literally "fatheads," whose visages are comical yet disturbing (most are drawn from religious and folkloric sources, though a growing trend is to caricature celebrities).

April: On **Día de Sant Jordi** (St. George's Day) every April 23, there's a particularly relaxed feeling, day and night, to the whole city. Traditionally, men gave their love a rose and women gave their special man a book (both are appropriate gifts, since this is also the birthday of Cervantes and Shakespeare). These days this tradition is not as strictly typed by gender, nor is it reserved solely for lovers. Rose sellers and book stalls spring up on sidewalks like mushrooms in a forest, and the city is full of people with the gifts in their hands.

June: **Día de Sant Joan** (St. John the Baptist's Day) on June 24 is celebrated with a *nit del foc,* when, to mark the summer solstice, locals paint themselves with blazing colors, build bonfires on the street corners, send up firecrackers through the night, and drink *cava* until they practically explode. At midnight, there are spectacular displays of fireworks from the heights of both Montjuïc and Tibidabo, with huge crowds gathering for both.

July: As the weather warms, so do the festivals. The best is the three-week **Grec**, Barcelona's arts festival, with theater, music, and dance events happening around the city each night. In addition to local talent, headlining acts from around the world have recently included guitarists Paco de Lucia and John McLaughlin, and Van Morrison and Ray Charles. Information and tickets are available at Centre de Informacion de la Virreina (tel 301–41–98; La Rambla, 99; Liceu metro stop).

August: While most of the city closes down during this vacation month, there are celebrations in two barrios—the **Festa Major de Gràcia** and the **Festa Major de Sants.** The Gràcia festival (usually the third week of the month) is the best, with a party every night for a week, the streets lavishly decorated, and free music on outdoor stages sprinkled liberally throughout the neighborhood.

September: The 11th is Catalonia's national holiday, **La Diada Nacional de Catalonia**, commemorating Catalonia's stand against the Madrid government in 1714 (even though, of course, the Catalans lost that battle). Catalan flags are everywhere, and at night there are political speeches and outdoor concerts. September 17–24 is the week-long **Festa de la Mercé** in honor of Our Lady of Mercy, Barcelona's patron saint. There's a wonderful nighttime parade of fireworks and dragons, free music every night, a parade of Catalunya's trademark *gegants*, and lots of fun for all ages.

October: **Tots Sants** (All Saints) is celebrated not only as a religious holiday memorializing the dead; each year more and more Barcelonans adopt the U.S. custom of dressing in a wide variety of outlandish costumes and partying hard into the night.

November: This month is marked by the **Festival Internacional de Jazz de Barcelona** (tel. 447–12–90), which features local groups alongside international headliners, recently including the great west-African horn player Manu Dibango. Venues and exact dates vary from year to year.

December: The **Fira de Santa Llúcia** leads up to Christmas, beginning the second week of the month when booths are set up in front of the Sagrada Familia, selling everything needed to make a crèche, including that extremely curious and most Catalan item, the *caganer*—a figure squatting with pants down, and defecating—which is traditionally placed next to the manger wherein lies the Christ child. Most booths stay open until 9pm. **Christmas** and the day after, **Saint Stephen's Day**, are both holidays.

Gay and lesbian resources... Barcelona's best resource is **Sextienda** (tel 318–86–76; Rauric, 11; open Mon–Sat until 8:30pm), which in addition to stocking all the usual gay sex shop supplies has a bulletin board and useful handouts, including a map of gay Barcelona. Lesbians should check out the lovely bookstore **Cómplices** (tel 412–72–83; Cervantes, 2; open Mon–Sat until 8:30pm), run by a friendly, English-speaking staff. There's a bulletin board and much local information. **Coordinadora Gai-Lesbiana** (tel 237–08–69; Carolines, 13; open Mon–Fri until 9pm) is a clearinghouse for information (much of it in English) about many local gay and lesbian groups. Staffers speak English.

Mail... Most post offices are not open at night, but the **Lista de Correos** (*poste restante*, or general delivery) window of the main post office stays open until 10pm Monday through Friday and 8pm on Saturday (tel 318–38–31; Plaça Antoni López, 1). Bring your passport or they won't give you your mail, and it's a good idea to have your correspondents write your name in big block letters. The main post office is located a few blocks north of the Ramblas, across from the waterfront and the huge mosaic/ sculpture by Roy Lichtenstein. Stamps are available at any **Tabac**, open until 8pm. Postage for letters to the U.S. under 20 grams and for postcards is 114 ptas.

Money matters... The currency exchange places along the Ramblas are legitimate, and open at night, but you can do better at a bank during the day, unless you're changing at least $400, and even then you should comparison shop with care. (See also Down & Dirty for Madrid.)

Newspapers and magazines... Even if your Spanish won't get you through every nuance of an entire newspaper, give the local dailies a try. Their *cartelera* sections have the best entertainment, arts, and events listings you can get. Plus, if you're into paying for pleasure, the classifieds provide a wealth of people, straight and not, ready to satisfy you—and what they offer is not difficult to understand in any language. There are four dailies here—*La Vanguardia,* the city's oldest, and in the middle of the road politically; *El País,* a Madrid daily (something like the *New York Times* of Spain) that prints a Barcelona edition; *El Periódico,* the closest thing to *USA Today* and politically slightly left of *La Vanguardia;* and *El Mundo,* the latest Madrid daily to begin publishing a local edition, known for both its investigative work and its ties to the current conservative government.

The weekly *Guía del Ocio* lists many events, and features prominent ads for clubs with beds and showers on the premises. And don't overlook the kiosks on almost every corner—they're plastered with announcements of coming attractions. For the truly Spanish-challenged, there is a free monthly magazine in English, *Barcelona Metropolitan,* which has interesting articles on life in Barcelona as well as events listings. Because it's a monthly, its listings are limited, but it can be useful. It's available in many cinemas and bars and at the **North American Institute's** library (tel 209–27–11; Vía Augusta, 123). The library is open until 9pm, and offers many magazines, ranging from *Time* to *The Nation, The New Yorker* and *The Paris Review,* as well as the *International Herald Tribune* and the *Wall Street Journal.* English-language newspapers and magazines, particularly the *Herald Tribune* and *USA Today's* international edition, are available at most of the news kiosks in the center of the city.

Opening and closing times... Shops generally open around 9 or 10am, close at 1:30 or 2pm, reopen at 4 or 5pm, and close at 8 or 9pm, Monday through Saturday. Banks are open from 8:30am to 2pm.

Public transportation... The buses and metros of **Transports Municipals de Barcelona** (tel 318–

BARCELONA ⟨ DOWN AND DIRTY

70–74, until 9pm) comprise a decent and reasonably priced public transportation system. However, for a city that keeps such late hours, the metros and buses (except those with an *N* prefix to their numbers) stop absurdly early: 11pm during the week and 1am on Saturday and Sunday. Tickets are on sale both on buses and in metro stations. Also available in any metro station are 10-trip tickets, called *T-2s,* for the metro only, and *T-1s,* which you can use on either metro or bus. If you'll be here long enough to use them up, they're much more economical than single-trip tickets. A single costs 120 ptas. (a little less than $1), and a T-1 or T-2 will set you back just 740 ptas. Buses and metros are generally safe at any hour, and the underground stations are well-lit and generally secure. Even so, of course, vigilance should be increased as the hour grows later.

Smoking... It can be a serious shock for health-conscious North Americans to find that the Barcelonans still smoke anywhere and everywhere and that restaurants do not segregate smokers from non. You've been forewarned. If you like cigars, Cuban brands are available in any **Tabac.**

Taxis... Given the early shutdown of the buses and metro, it's a good thing taxis are also reasonably priced: 240 ptas. to start and it generally costs less than $5 for a typical ride of a couple of miles. Taxis are black and yellow and display a green light on top when they're empty. You can flag them down, find them at the stands marked with a big *T* in busy areas of town, or call one of the city's eight dispatch companies. Try **Barnataxi** (tel 357–77–55); **Taxi Radio Móvil** (tel 358–11–11); **Tele Taxi** (tel 392–22–22); or **Radio Taxi Metropolitana de Barcelona** (tel 300–38–11).

Telephone... The *Locutorio Telefónico* (see Down and Dirty for Madrid) at 88 La Rambla are open until 11pm daily; in the lobby of the Sants train station at Plaça Països Catalans they are available Monday through Saturday until 10:15pm and Sunday until 9pm. And at the **Estació d'Autobusos Barcelona-Nord** (Ali Bei, 80) you can phone home until 11pm Monday through Friday. When calling Barcelona from other parts of Spain, first dial 93 (Barcelona's area code). When calling from the States, first dial 34 (the country code for Spain), then 3 (the city code for Barcelona).

Tickets... Ticket buying is easy at the **Servi-Caixa** machines conveniently located in the **La Caixa** banks. They offer seats for a wide range of theater, music, and sports events, they take credit cards and have instructions in English, and, best of all, they don't tack on a service charge. There is a fee when you charge your tickets via **Tel-Entrades** (tel 902–10–12–12). For those who prefer to buy tickets in person, there are ticket brokers' offices at unit 65, 56 Passeig de Gràcia, and at the corner of Gran Vía and Calle Aribau in the Plaça Universitat.

Time... See Down & Dirty for Madrid.

Tipping... See Down & Dirty for Madrid.

Tourist information... The central office of **Turisme de Barcelona** (tel. 304–31–35; open daily until 9pm) is underground in the Plaça Catalunya, across from the department store El Corte Inglés; there's also a branch at the airport (tel 478–47–04; open Mon–Sat until 8:30pm). During the summer, tourist aides in red jackets roam the Ramblas until 9pm each day to answer questions. In addition, there's a tourist information booth at the waterfront across from the foot of the Ramblas (open daily until 9pm).

Traveling for the disabled... Many a disgruntled Para-Olympic athlete was heard to disparage Barcelona during the 1992 Games for its absolute lack of accessibility. That is changing. Buildings recently constructed, ranging from libraries to museums to cinemas, have wheelchair-accessible entrances and adapted bathrooms. As older buses are replaced in the city's fleet, the new ones are equipped to handle wheelchairs. Still a far cry from a truly accessible city, there is, at least, a growing consciousness that, we can hope, will make the city more accessible in the years to come.

MADRID/BARCELONA ☾ INDEX